Understanding Teenagers

SOMETIMES WILD, ALWAYS WISE

D0412872

Understanding Teenagers

SOMETIMES WILD, ALWAYS WISE

Tony Humphreys and Helen Ruddle

Gill & Macmillan

Gill & Macmillan
Hume Avenue, Park West
Dublin 12
with associated companies throughout the world
www.gillmacmillan.ie
© Tony Humphreys and Helen Ruddle 2012

ISBN: 978 07171 5390 9

Print origination by O'K Graphic Design, Dublin
Printed by ScandBook AB, Sweden
Index by Cover to Cover

This book is typeset in Agfa Rotis Sans Serif 10.5pt on 13.5pt

*To all the parents and young people
whose stories inspired
the writing of this book.*

Also by Tony Humphreys and Helen Ruddle

Books by Tony Humphreys and Helen Ruddle
The Compassionate Intentions of Illness
Relationship, Relationship, Relationship: The Heart of a Mature Society

Books by Tony Humphreys
Self-Esteem, the Key to Your Child's Future
Leaving the Nest: What Families are all About
The Power of 'Negative' Thinking
Myself, My Partner
Work and Worth: Balancing Your Life
A Different Kind of Teacher
A Different Kind of Discipline
Whose Life are you Living?
The Mature Manager: Managing from Inside Out
All About Children: Questions Parents Ask
Leadership with Consciousness

CDs by Tony Humphreys
Raising Your Child's Self-Esteem
Self-Esteem for Adults
Work and Self

Books by Helen Ruddle
O'Connor, J., Ruddle, H., and O'Gallagher, M., *Caring for the Elderly, Part II: The Caring Process: A Study of Carers in the Home*
O'Connor, J., Ruddle, H., and O'Gallagher, M., *Cherished Equally? Educational and Behavioural Adjustment of Children*
O'Connor, J., and Ruddle, H., *You Can Do It: A Life Skills Book for Women*
O'Connor, J., Ruddle, H., and O'Gallagher, M., *Sheltered Housing in Ireland: Its Role and Contribution in the Care of the Elderly*
O'Connor, J., and Ruddle, H., *Business Matters for Women*

O'Connor, J., and Ruddle, H., *Breaking the Silence, Violence in the Home: The Woman's Perspective*

Ruddle, H., *Strengthening Family Communication to Prevent Misuse of Alcohol and Drugs: An Evaluation Study*

Ruddle, H., Donoghue, F., and Mulvihill, R., *The Years Ahead: A Review of the Implementation of its Recommendations*

Ruddle, H., and Mulvihill, R., *Reaching Out: Charitable Giving and Volunteering in the Republic of Ireland – The 1997/98 Survey*

Ruddle, H., Prizeman, G., and Jaffro, G., *Evaluation of Local Drugs Task Force Projects*

Ruddle, H., Prizeman, G., Haslett, D., Mulvihill, R., and Kelly, E., *Meeting the Health and Social Services Information Needs of Older People*

Contents

CHAPTER ONE

Beginnings: A vision for the teenage years

A dolescence is about starting the process of becoming independent and self-reliant and, depending on the young person's experiences in infancy and childhood, the teenage years can be a rollercoaster of emotional highs and lows or a relatively smooth ride into maturity.

It is important to distinguish between being an adult and being mature; it is not the passing of years per se that brings about independence and self-reliance, and being of adult years is no guarantee of maturity. Children who move into their adolescent years with considerable fears, insecurities and doubts about their worth will find facing the challenges involved – emotional, social, sexual, intellectual, educational and career – very difficult. These adolescents will find powerful and creative ways of postponing or avoiding these challenges; they may be '*wild*' in their presenting behaviours. Parents, teachers, and other concerned adults may view with alarm the young person's seemingly irresponsible and difficult behaviours, but it is the adult who possesses maturity, who will see a deeper reality that needs to be resolved for the troubled, and troubling, young people to progress towards self-realisation.

A belief that will echo throughout this book is that young people who present with challenging and difficult responses are not out to make life difficult for others, but they are trying to show how difficult life is for them; they are being '*wise*'. Attention to what lies hidden behind their distressing responses is what is required for these teenagers to begin to make the progress towards mature adulthood that they, in their wisdom, want to make.

Regrettably, often the very adults who are best placed to respond to the wise manifestations of these teenagers are not in a mature place themselves. Adults who are in turmoil themselves cannot recognise the underlying wisdom and tend to respond to adolescents' troubling responses with blame, exasperation, aggression, over-protection, ridicule and, perhaps, denial. All of these responses mirror the inner insecurities of the adults and, sadly, their defensive responses serve only to escalate the distress being experienced by the young people around them. In this situation, teenagers will rightly feel that adults do not understand them and they are pushed further into seeking comfort and protection from their often equally troubled peers. Of course, what the teenagers cannot yet consciously see is that those parents, teachers and other adults who respond defensively to them need as much, and often more, understanding and help than the teenagers themselves.

This book seeks to help parents, and other significant adults in the lives of teenagers, to uncover the wisdom beneath troubled and troublesome behaviours exhibited by young people. The first step always is for the adults to become consciously aware of their own troubled and troublesome responses and to seek resolution of their own inner insecurities.

A not uncommon response on the part of parents, and other adults such as teachers, is to seek a psychiatric or psychological label for young people's challenging behaviours. The most common labels include attention deficit disorder, attention deficit with hyperactivity disorder, oppositional defiance disorder, Asperger syndrome, obsessive compulsive disorder and dyslexia. The assumption is that these syndromes have their source in biochemical, neurological or genetic factors, and treatment often involves medication. But parents, and other concerned adults, need to be aware that there are other approaches to challenging behaviours that differ greatly from the 'disorder' model; approaches that focus on the overall psychosocial context of the young person's life. This book is based on the latter model and adopts the stance that all behaviour has meaning and purpose when understood in the context of the person's life story and the network of relationships in which she or he is involved. This book rests on psychological foundations that recognise that insecurities and vulnerabilities have their source in early relationships and, accordingly, it is through relationships that resolution occurs.

There is research to show that between 20-25 per cent of adolescents experience considerable undetected turmoil. Ironically, it is often their peers who recognise their fears and insecurities but peers are not in a position to provide what the young person most wants – unconditional love. In this book, we provide guidelines on the kind of unconditionally loving relating that children and young people need, in the various holding worlds of which they are part, if they are to feel safe to give open and real, rather than defensive, expression to the different dimensions of self – emotional, intellectual, behavioural, physical, sexual, social, creative and spiritual. The term 'holding world' refers to the network of relationships within a particular social context – starting with the womb and extending into family community, school, workplace and wider society. When adult, your own relationship with yourself becomes the ultimate holding world.

The manifestations of adolescent insecurity that tend to most distress parents are those that can be described as 'acting-out' behaviours; the most common examples of which include:

- argumentativeness
- verbal aggression
- physical violence
- refusal to co-operate
- school phobia, school refusal, school dropout
- lack of educational motivation
- self-harming
- suicidal thoughts
- anorexia nervosa, bulimia, over-eating
- non-conformist clothing
- body piercing, tattoos
- drug taking
- drunkenness
- stealing
- emotional withdrawal
- social withdrawal
- shyness
- self-consciousness
- constant rebelliousness
- sexual activity inappropriate for their age.

What parents and other adults often miss is that those adolescents who are over-dedicated to their studies, who thrive on success and who dread failure, who 'keep their head down' and never cause any trouble – adolescents who can be described as 'acting-in' their turmoil – are often more at risk than their 'acting-out' peers by missing out on vital emotional and social aspects of adolescent development. Sadly, because the 'acting-in' behaviours of conformity, addiction to success, and attempts to gain recognition through performance and achievements do not pose threats to the worlds of parents and teachers, these flags of inner turmoil are often flown in vain. Another flag of inner distress often flown in vain by young people is illness; illness usually being responded to solely in physical ways without recognition of the equally important need for emotional responsiveness.

In this book, we seek to help adults understand that every teenager has a unique life-story and that the protective strategies a particular teenager develops will match perfectly the particular circumstances of that life-story; flags of distress can look very different from one teenager to another – some will be of an 'acting-in' nature, some of an 'acting-out' nature and some will involve physical embodiment.

The book emphasises that in responding to teenagers' challenging behaviours, parents, teachers and other adults need to appreciate that no matter how difficult the young person's behaviour, it is creative and always makes sense. Appreciation of the wisdom of what is often termed 'problematic' behaviour by itself goes a long way towards helping the young person to resolve what is troubling him or her. Reactions such as judgement, condemnation, labelling, blaming or throwing up one's arms in despair, only pose further threats in the already unsafe holding world that is contributing to the adolescent turmoil. Parents, and other adults, are in a better position to respond with understanding and compassion when they understand and recognise the wisdom and meaning of their own defensive responses.

An important consideration when responding to the challenging behaviours of adolescents is to evaluate whether the presenting behaviours are 'new' or 'persistent'. It is inevitable that teenagers will experience 'new' difficulties as they become part of wider holding worlds. Most of these difficulties will resolve themselves through experiences of trial and error, peer support, the passage of time, and the encouragement and support of adults, particularly parents and teachers. When the difficulties are of a 'persistent' nature – stretching back into childhood and continuing into adolescence – then it is a more serious matter that urgently requires compassionate and determined responsiveness. Attention, too, needs to be given to the frequency, intensity, duration and persistence over time of the challenging responses (this also applies to the behaviours of the significant adults in their lives). For example, the adolescent who steals several times in a week needs considerably more help than the one who has only ever stolen once. The amount stolen is an important mirror of the teenager's hidden distress as is the answer to the question: how long has this stealing being going on – six months, a year or several years? In terms of aggression or sulking or withdrawal or other such symptoms, the question of how long the response endures in the presenting situation is an important clue to the level of distress – is it one minute, five minutes, an hour, several hours, a day, a week, a month?

In helping young people progress down the path to maturity, we propose that there are certain understandings that all adults, but particularly parents, teachers and other significant adults – for example, grandparents, club leaders, sports trainers – need to have; the more important of which include:

- the nature of the self and the development of self-esteem, both in oneself and in children and adolescents
- the wise purposes of the various stages that teenagers go through
- the crucial process of finding realness and authenticity
- the key factors involved in the preparation of young people for adult maturity
- the adult defensive behaviours that pose threats to the wellbeing of young people
- the issues that adults who are troubled and troubling need to resolve
- the identification of the signs of inner distress during the teenage years
- the best ways to respond to 'new' and 'persistent' teenage problems in living
- the wisdom and creativity of what traditionally have been known as 'problems', 'maladaptive behaviours' or 'dysfunctions' but what are more accurately seen as 'substitute' (as opposed to real) responses to threats to wellbeing
- the nature of parental 'letting go' of young adult children, and teenagers' 'leave-taking' of their parents.

This book emphasises that the nature of the relationship that the parent, teacher or other significant adult has with the young person is critical to the resolution of any presenting difficulties. Indeed, the very source of the young person's distress may very well be the nature of the relationships experienced with significant adults. The helping relationship needs to be unconditionally loving, compassionate, non-judgemental, empathic and genuine. It is consistent relating of this kind that creates the safety for the young person to begin to consciously identify what is troubling him or her and, with the support and encouragement of parents, teachers and, where necessary, a counsellor, to seek resolution of what has lain hidden. It is almost always the case that parents need to reflect on their own ways of relating to themselves, to each other and to each of their children. Parents do well to hold on to the reality that each child in a family has a different mother and a different father and that children are ingenious in developing their own individual and creative responses to the kind of relating they experience from each of their parents.

In this book, we emphasise that the creation of 'safe holding' – essentially unconditionally loving relating – is an integral part of the parenting and educating of children. This 'holding' needs to be there for the various expressions of self – physical, sexual, emotional, social, intellectual, behavioural and creative. The nature of safe holding for these different expressions is examined, so that adults who have responsibilities towards young people can engage in best practice of these responsibilities. Essentially, safe holding involves the creation of patient, nurturing, secure, encouraging and non-threatening responses to the young person's self-expressions. It will be clear in the book that such holding is not a licence for young people to do what they like, but a development of responsible freedom. A useful rule of thumb with regard to the development of responsible self-expression is that 'the more responsibility shown, the more freedom given'. Many young people resent the fact that parents are responsible for their total welfare up to their eighteenth year and need – and deserve – to know where they are, whom they are with, what they are doing and what time they will be home. When adolescents do not co-operate with the responsibilities of parents, the parents need to maintain very definite boundaries around their own wellbeing; a challenge that can seem daunting but is in fact an act of love that, as this book shows, is attainable.

The book is structured so that each chapter stands on its own, enabling the reader to focus in on specific issues that may arise in their own and in their teenagers' lives:

- The wisdom of the processes taking place in adolescence (Chapter 2)
- Parents' own sense of self (Chapter 3)
- Parents parenting themselves (Chapter 4)
- Key dimensions of the parenting of teenagers (Chapter 5)
- Creating safety for the expression of individuality (Chapter 6)
- The creation of boundaries with teenagers (Chapter 7)
- Safe holding for teenagers in their sexual expression (Chapter 8)
- Safe holding for teenagers in the school holding world (Chapter 9)
- Responding to teenagers who are troubled and troubling (Chapter 10)
- Responding to teenage addictions (Chapter 11)
- Responding to teenager given a psychiatric label (Chapter 12)
- Responding to teenage depression, extreme shyness, self-harming and suicide (Chapter 13)
- Creating safe holding for teenagers to leave the nest and for their parents to let them go (Chapter 14).

Whilst this book is primarily directed towards parents, teachers, counsellors and other adults who have charge over young people, it is a book that older adolescents certainly could read, not only to enlighten themselves on what the passage through adolescence is all about, but also to assess to what degree their parents and other significant adults have achieved a strong sense of self, a solid interior life and strong sense of self-realisation.

CHAPTER TWO

The wisdom of the teenage years

- The challenge of independence
- Stages on the way to independence
- 'Adults know nothing': A wise illusion of teenagers
- Being your real self: A key challenge for teenagers
- Threats for teenagers against being their real selves
- How parents can help teenagers find the safety to be real
- Teenagers want to belong

The challenge of independence

With the coming of the teenage years, a young person starts to move out from the earlier, narrower holding worlds of childhood into the wider worlds of education, friendship, community and, possibly, work. This move into wider worlds brings with it many new challenges and possible threats, but adolescence is also the time when the person has the possibility of starting the process of independence – starting the process where the self becomes the ultimate holding world.

In her early years, the child is completely dependent on the adults in her life – particularly her parents. Clearly, the child is dependent physically but at a more profound level the child is dependent on her parents for love, visibility, recognition and a sense of her capability; she is dependent on her parents for safe holding '*to be*' in the world. The child, from very early on, will already have had an unconscious awareness of any threats present in her holding worlds; she will have learned how 'to be' for her parents, how 'to fit around' them – this may involve rebellion, but the parents are still at the centre of the child's life. The child will have developed her own particular protective strategies for managing whatever threats were experienced; she will have developed a '*screen self*' that has enabled her to fit with, and have a sense of belonging with, the most important people in her life – her parents, on whom she is utterly dependent to know her worth, lovability and capability. Depending on the nature of these early relationships, a child's screen self will manifest how much of her real self is emotionally safe for her to show.

With the coming of adolescence and the move into wider holding worlds, the young person need no longer be so dependent on her parents in order to know consciously who she really is – a person who is unconditionally lovable, powerful and unique. The crucial process in the teenage years is about starting to become your own person; it is about becoming independent; it is about taking responsibility for yourself and your own actions; it is about finding the safety to be true to yourself, to be authentic. It is important to recognise that the teenager is only at the beginning of what is, in effect, a life-long process. Becoming independent does not happen simply with the passing of years; indeed, there are many adults who are not in a solid place of self-realisation and realness. Sadly, neither are such adults – parents, teachers, others in charge of young people – in a mature place to guide young people towards establishing independence and self-realisation. Clearly, when teenagers do not have adults in their lives who model maturity, it is difficult for them to make progress towards independence. The reality is that the very people teenagers need to support and aid them in their pursuit of independence are often struggling for independence themselves. It is unusual for a young person to find a model of independence among her peer group and so the co-dependent relationships that have been part and parcel of family and school life are repeated with peers.

Young people have a dawning consciousness of the challenges that face them as they trek the terrain of their teenage years and, wisely, they usually approach these challenges in a staged manner. The challenges are primarily concerned with finding their own particular ways of giving open and real expression to the several dimensions of self – emotional, physical, behavioural, intellectual, social, sexual and creative. The fact that the central challenge in adolescence is about finding realness and authenticity is often missed by parents and teachers, who overemphasise academic and career progress to the detriment of the more profound challenges young people face.

The onset of adolescence is marked outwardly by physical changes;

the more obvious being breast development and menstruation in girls, and beard development, voice breaking and wet dreams among boys. These physical changes happen automatically and are outward manifestations of the shift from childhood to adulthood. The outward physical changes enable the development of certain elements of independence but it is the inner shift – from childhood dependence on others for a sense of self to independence – that is the more crucial process.

While accommodation of physical changes can bring its own challenges, the more important challenges are concerned with changes in the inner world of a young person. A key change is that the young person is faced with letting go of the relative safety of the childhood holding worlds of home and community – primary school, church, neighbourhood – and moving into the wider and much more challenging holding worlds of adulthood – such as second- and third-level education, the workplace, and wider society. The ultimate challenge for the young person is to reach that stronghold where she looks to herself as her primary holding world. Maturity means having a sense of your own unique person, becoming self-realised, being emotionally and socially independent, establishing your own beliefs and values, carving out educational and career paths that realise your particular intellectual and creative potential, and establishing financial independence. There are also the challenges of creating friendship relationships with same and opposite gender peers, and the exploration and development of intimacy with another person.

Given the enormity of the challenges involved, it is no wonder that many teenagers create substitute behaviours – such as rebellion or withdrawal – in order to reduce their fears. Young people whose earlier holding worlds have enabled the continuous development of a strong sense of self will take on the challenges, not necessarily with ease, but certainly with determination. Those adolescents who bring lack of confidence and lack of competence from their childhood years will struggle with the demands of becoming independent and may carry these struggles into their older adult years, even into old age.

In order to meet the challenges arising from the search for realness and independence, and from participation in the wider holding worlds of adult life, young people unconsciously attempt to create opportunities to establish their independence. There is a realisation among young people that further supports *beyond* the family are required – a development that parents can feel threatened by – but there is also a knowing that parents' influence is still a major factor in their lives. Of course, the nature of that influence is determined by the individual parent's present level of maturity; parents are effective in supporting independence in their sons and daughters only to the extent to which they themselves demonstrate independence. When the road to independence has been paved from the early years of childhood, adolescents take on the extra responsibilities of adult life with relative ease. When a child has not been given age-appropriate opportunities to stand on her own two capable feet – due to being over-protected or over-controlled – then the path to independence will prove difficult.

Stages on the way to independence

There is a wonderful wisdom in the staged way that the teenager attempts to reach independence; recognition of this wisdom by parents and other significant adults is a very important support for the young person. The early stages of adolescence are marked by gender polarisation in interactions with others – boys with boys and girls with girls. This is often referred to as the *gang* phase or the *group homosexual* phase. The intelligence of this phase of the process of independence is that young people need to discover whether members of their own gender will back them up in the much wider world into which they have entered. The qualities of loyalty and co-operation come to prominence during this time. Conformity – dressing and looking the same as one another – is common during this phase. The purpose of peer conformity is to establish a group identity that is different from that of adults – the very adults from whom the adolescents need to find independence. Identifying with the group is a way, too, of a teenager postponing the much more difficult challenge of establishing her own individuality. There is always the possibility of being excluded by some of your peers, but the 'gang' provides the security of having others who will provide support in times of crisis. Towards the end of this gender-polarised group phase, the establishment of the 'bosom pal' of the same gender begins to emerge. It is a clever movement to have a 'bosom pal' of the same gender with whom the teenager can talk safely about anything; things she would not discuss even with the other gang members or with her parents. Often the bosom pal becomes a life-long friend and an enduring source of support. The value of friendship in supporting independence and self-realisation is discovered through the bosom-pal relationship.

Around mid-adolescence, there occurs a *transition* phase. This is largely concerned with the challenge of checking out the other half of the population – the opposite gender – to see what level of support can be found from them when taking on the challenges of the adult world. The problem here is that, up to now, the opposite gender was 'off limits' – girls saw boys as rough and uncouth and boys saw girls as silly and 'frilly' – and now the teenager has to climb down from this rigid, earlier stance and open up to the potential of friendship with members of the opposite gender. The value of encompassing within yourself the different qualities often described as 'feminine' and 'masculine' is discovered through these opposite-gender friendships.

This transition time is typically marked by 'moodiness'; partly due to the embarrassing capitulation needed to attract members of the opposite gender, but also because time is moving on and more adult responsibilities are coming the teenager's way. It is important that parents and teachers realise the sensitivities of this time in an adolescent's world and that they do not personalise the teenager's moodiness as a rejection of them. Staying on the sidelines and offering support from there is what is needed. Any attempt to intrude into her inner world by demanding to know what is going on will only further alienate the young person. Tolerating moodiness does not mean accepting any show of aggression or disrespect but it is essential to remember that the young person does not deliberately want to upset or cause hurt, but is struggling within herself. Any behaviour that is of a threatening nature towards others needs to be challenged firmly, but calmly and without judgement and in a manner that does not jeopardise the relationship between the adult and the teenager. When adults *react* to a teenager's difficult behaviours, such *reactions* can be even more threatening than the behaviours of the young person. Reaction provides no resolution and the unhappy situation only escalates.

Moving on from friendships, in the next phase, the teenager begins to explore the possibility of more intimate relationships. For any particular teenager, the orientation may be towards a same-gender or opposite-gender intimate relationship. It can be very difficult for teenagers to make a free choice in this regard, as all the pressure is towards the development of an opposite-gender relationship. It can be quite dangerous for a young person to follow a choice for same-gender relationships, and to do so, she needs very safe holding in her family, school and friendship worlds (see Chapter 8). At this stage, teenagers tend to be 'promiscuous'; the wisdom of this being to check out how many are likely to provide support in the future. This promiscuity does not spring from insensitivity or from lack of caring, nor is it intended to cause hurt to others; its purpose is to ascertain the level of security that is to be had among peers. For the young person with low self-esteem, great hurt can arise when the other person's attraction proves to be short-lived, and the ending of the relationship can be experienced as emotional rejection. Parents need to be vigilant for signs of over-involvement in any particular relationship in the early teenage years. Sexual conquest is not the aim of this phase, but the number of young people attracted is important.

Eventually, the need for a more enduring one-to-one relationship emerges and this heralds the onset of the *romantic* phase (akin to the bosom pal). Again, at this stage, it is friendship that matters most – sexual interaction is often not on the agenda, or at least is not the priority. At this stage, a young person wants to experience a fully intimate relationship – a soul-mate – not with any intention of being together in marriage, but with the intention of having one person in her life on whom she can rely totally. This reliance on another is the precursor of independence; an ambition that can take considerable effort over time to accomplish. At this stage, adolescents 'in love' tend to idolise each other, 'warts and all'. For many teenagers, the in-love experience tends to be short-lived because, inevitably, the insecurities and doubts that have been masked begin to come to the surface. A young person with low self-esteem will cling for dear life to such a relationship and, when it ends, she is likely to be devastated, even sometimes to the point of suicide. The adolescent who leans on the intimate relationship as a life-saver will not have experienced strong and supportive relationships within the family holding world and is unlikely to have developed a bosom pal. But the reality that young people have to face is that we can save only our own lives and dependence on another puts us at high risk. Unless the young person resolves her vulnerabilities – whatever their extent and depth –

through the formation of a strong sense of herself, intimate relationships with others will continue to be troubled.

'Adults know nothing': A wise illusion of teenagers

Mark Twain made the wonderful observation that: 'When I was 18 I believed my parents knew nothing and when I was 20 I couldn't believe how much they had learned in two years.'

In their late teens, young people can be utterly convinced that they 'know it all', that they are the ones who are going to save the world while adults just 'haven't a clue'. Some people label this simply as an idealistic phase that young people on the brink of their adult years go through, but there is more to it than that and, in truth, there is sound reason underlying this illusion. In speaking with teenagers, it emerges how absolutely unready they are for the responsibilities, demands, upsets and rollercoaster ride of mature adulthood. It is wise and clever of teenagers to create unconsciously the illusion that they know everything in the face of what can seem like overwhelming responsibilities. The illusion enables them not to run away and, indeed, sends them headlong into a world where 'angels fear to tread'. This headlong plunge into the presenting challenges makes it more likely that the young illusionist will learn from her experiences and, like Mark Twain, eventually become a realist; parents need to recognise that what the young person is doing is creating opportunities for mature development. The armoury of the illusion means that the teenager neither looks for help nor do they welcome being advised about what to do. Parents would do well to see the 'vice' in 'advice' and, rather than advising, show belief in the young person's capability and intelligence and encourage her to reach her own answers.

When, out of fear, adolescents avoid the necessary emotional, sexual, intellectual, occupational, social and spiritual challenges of adult life, they can find themselves stuck in dependence, with life being very limited for them. The choice of the avoidance path is also wise as it signals that there were experiences of major threat in earlier holding worlds, and that the young person is not even remotely psycho-socially ready for adulthood. Resolution of the abandonment persisting from childhood is required before the safety to proceed to maturity will emerge.

Understandably, parents can experience great frustration with what they perceive to be headstrong, arrogant and irrational behaviour. It helps if parents, rather than blaming the young person, own their own responses as being about themselves – their frustration is about their need for the young person to make the 'right' decisions, to be sensible and to listen to and avail of the parents' experiences. There is a saying 'you can't put an old head on young shoulders' and indeed it is not wise to even try. It is the mature parent who allows the adolescent to learn from her own experiences and who recognises that teenagers are not here to live their parents' lives but must, instead, follow their own unique paths. Parents who find this hard to accept will exclaim 'we're only saying this for your own good', but, in truth, they are saying it for their own defensive purposes. Some parents defend their intrusiveness by saying, 'we're only trying to protect him from making the wrong decision', but implicit in this is the message that only the parents know what is 'right', and there is an underlying demand to see and do things the parents' way. When parents view teenagers as being 'arrogant' and 'irrational', they are revealing their own defensive arrogance of believing they know what is best for the teenager and their own defensive 'irrationality' whereby they do not see that teenagers need the space and the support to learn from their own lived experiences.

Within the boundary of maintaining their own dignity and self-respect, parents can best respond to a teenager's illusion of knowing it all with a silent understanding of the wisdom of the illusion, with continuing to relate unconditionally, with waiting on the sideline for the teenager to come to them for help and support, and with manifest belief that she will come through this very challenging time of her life. The presence of unconditional love and belief are the two critical supports needed, not only for the teenagers but also for the parents.

Parents sometimes ask: 'How do I respond when my teenage daughter declares that, "School is stupid, teachers are ancient and know nothing, poetry is useless."?' It is crucial that the parent does not get trapped into conflict with the teenager by attempting to argue how ridiculous she is being in what she is saying. Maturity calls for an open response such as, 'I hear what you are saying and I'm wondering how things are for you in school?' A likely response is, 'I just hate school and I want to be out working and making lots of money.' The secret is to return responsibility to the young person for what she is saying; in this way, the focus stays on her and the decision-making lies with her. This process of uncovering the real hidden issue is likely to take time and patience. The truth that may eventually emerge could be, 'I know little or nothing about life.' When this truth is present, a parent can then affirm how much she knows about what it is like to be on the brink of adulthood and can show her willingness to offer the support and resources that will best enable her daughter to negotiate this particular time of her life.

Being yourself: A key challenge for teenagers

During their childhood, the key challenge for teenagers had been to find a 'fit' with their parents. As teenagers begin to expand their relationship networks beyond the family, the key challenge now is to start becoming their own person; to start the process of acting from a real place rather than from the screen self. The ultimate goal is for the teenager to form a secure and strong sense of their unique self; this sense of self has a critical influence upon their ability to form relationships and effectively manage all the responsibilities of adult life. In order to start the process of discovering who they are as unique individuals, teenagers go through a process of questioning; for example, questioning how they feel about relationships, religion, spirituality and career, and questioning their values, beliefs and ethics. Finding answers to such questions is not what ultimately provides a secure sense of self, but it does provide the beginnings of some sense of being one's own person.

Teenagers who already have developed a strong screen self – arising from their experiences in early holding worlds of home, classrooms, schools and community – will struggle with finding their own answers to these questions. These teenagers experience confusion around who they really are; an experience that some psychologists refer to as a *confused identity*. Teenagers with no definite sense of self will often try out different 'identities' – particularly the characteristics of idols, such as soccer players, musicians, singers, a teacher, peer, uncle or aunt whom they admire – in an attempt to see what might fit for them. This is a wise exploration but one that needs to be concluded at some stage in later adolescence. The young person who already has a strong sense of her unique self – whose screen is not so strongly entrenched – will not experience such painful levels of confusion and will find it easier to reach her own answers and conclusions around the questions that arise.

Teenagers who are in deep inner turmoil tend to stay confused and carry that confusion into their adulthood. Insecurity and uncertainty dog their steps and affect everything they do. These adolescents are understandably very frightened, which can give rise to moodiness, anger and depression, as if they are trapped in some dark prison from which they cannot escape.

Some adolescents do *not* go through the rebelliousness and confusion that can signal the attempt to find one's real self but, instead, continue to 'fit around' and identify with their parents and any other significant adults who posed threats in their earlier holding worlds; this position is referred to by some writers as a *crystallised* identity. This 'crystallisation' is a wise process in the face of emotional perils such as rejection, diminishment, humiliation and hypercriticism. In the face of such experiences, the young person unconsciously – and very wisely – concludes that conformity is the best strategy and chooses to suspend her own individuality. There are many families where young people feel compelled to follow in their parents' professional footsteps – being, for example, a farmer, doctor, teacher, business person, nurse or working in the family business. It can be very difficult for a son or daughter to rebel against such parental expectations when there are threats of being isolated and exiled as being troubled, troublesome and ungrateful. But, if truth be voiced – which is unlikely within such families – the young people who do conform are more at risk that those who rebel.

When a young person, out of fear, goes against her own unique nature and conforms to a parent's projections rather than living her own life, she will experience continuous underlying feelings of oppression and resentment. What also persists is the fear, sometimes terror, of disappointing or letting down her parents, and so there can be no peace and contentment. If the young person with a crystallised sense of self gets married and has children, the likelihood is that the dark pattern will repeat. Young people who live out the parents' projections need a strong supportive relationship that champions and encourages them to live their own individual lives. The emergence of such a u-turn is highly challenging; enduring support is required to bring about the freedom to be self and to create one's own life path.

Of course, the young person in a threatening family holding world who rebels against parental pressures is also at risk; she will experience confusion and because there is no support and safety within the family to resolve this confusion, she will continue to be lost to self well into adulthood. There is no possibility of resolution, unless she finds support and safety in a relationship *outside* the family. Sometimes, there is a need for psychotherapy, where the necessary relationship depth can be provided for the young person to safely explore the question: 'Who am I really?'

Threats for teenagers against being their real selves

The word 'confusion' accurately describes the struggles that adolescents go through, particularly in the late teenage years. These young people are attempting to fuse or connect with their own individuality, but there are many forces that make it difficult to come into that inner stronghold.

Adolescents who have had the enormous advantage of having been loved for themselves, and not having to prove themselves through their behaviours – academic or otherwise – generally manage to resolve any sense of confusion by early adulthood. However, because consistent unconditional love is a rare phenomenon, the vast majority of adolescents experience some confusion, ranging from mild to severe, around the important question: 'Who's my real self?' There are adolescents who do not come to any conclusions about this question, and they carry their confusion into their adult years. Some adults, too, never resolve their inner confusion, and carry their doubts and insecurities to the grave.

What creates such confusion? The first, and very powerful, factor is the level of inner security the adolescent brings from childhood; the insecure child becomes the confused teenager. A second powerful influence is the level of wellbeing within the family holding world. A stable family situation has the capacity to hold and support in a non-intrusive way the turmoil the teenager may be experiencing; such family stability is largely determined by the psycho-social wellbeing of the parents (or parent in single-parent families). If parents have not found their own sense of self, they do not have the necessary security to create the safe environment for their offspring to know themselves and be independent.

Another factor that makes it tremendously difficult for adolescents to find peace with themselves and others is the amount of unresolved conflict present in their families. The family that calmly, openly and systematically resolves differences between family members acts as a model for young people, showing them how they can best sort out their own inner conflicts. The essential aspect of effective conflict-resolution is *uninterrupted active listening*. This type of listening allows each person to state what is upsetting her, and the other parties to the conflict know they will get the same opportunity to voice their side of things. Sadly, what is far more common within families is *interrupted listening*, where the listeners start defending themselves as soon as a few words have been spoken. Once defensiveness occurs, there is little chance of resolving conflict. Preaching to or advising young people is a defensive response many parents fall into and it only adds to the inner turmoil of the young person and escalates interpersonal conflict.   i0 3⊦, 53٩ | 6⊦٩ · 12⊃

The school environment is another major influence on the confusion experienced by teenagers. Schools that emphasise academic performance above personal development do not provide the safe holding needed for young people to work through their confusions; indeed, such schools create further threat. It is the school with the mission of providing holistic education, and that considers the inner security of a student as far more important than academic knowledge, that creates the dynamic and healing environment that enables young people to resolve their identity crises. Sending young people out into the world of third-level education, training or work with a strong sense of their own selves is the greatest gift that schools can provide for their students. Sadly, only few schools view education in this way. But then policy makers, school principals and teachers need to ask themselves the question: 'Have I come to a place of peace about who I am and what am I doing in this world?'

Many parents and teachers blame the young person's peer group for her problems in living. This is 'passing the buck' because the peer group is the coming together of young people who are struggling with the essential questions, and how they are with each other is very similar to how people relate to each other within their respective families and classrooms. Societal change never comes through children and adolescents – the future of society, and, indeed, of young people, always lies in the hands of adults.

How parents can help teenagers find the safety to be real

Below are some suggestions about what parents can do to help their sons and daughters find the safety to be real and authentic. Parents can aspire to relate to their teenage sons and daughters as outlined below, but parents need to have compassion, understanding and empathy for themselves too and allow that they may not always meet aspirations; it is important to remember that effort and commitment count, and parents do not have to be perfect, just 'good enough'. Any falling back from aspirations can be seen as an opportunity for parents to reflect on the question: 'Who is the real me?'

Parents can aspire to:

- reflect on their own sense of self and on whether or not they are still in a place of confusion; if they are, they need to seek relevant help (see chapters 3 and 4)
- express unconditional love for their son or daughter; if they struggle with this, it is essential to find ways of resolving this struggle
- ensure communication is of a direct and clear nature and allow the adolescents to come to their own decisions
- actively listen, without interruption, and be open to differences between them and their teenagers
- value and respect (even though they may not agree with) the opinions of their adolescents
- find ways of getting to know what adolescence is all about
- express belief in their teenagers' capacity to make their own decisions and manage the complexities of adulthood
- be specific, in their interactions with their adolescents, both in their praising of particular efforts to be responsible and in challenging actions that may threaten the adolescents' wellbeing
- stay emotionally present at key times – morning time, meal times, bedtime; a sense of belonging is critical to the development of a strong identity
- be open about their own feelings, thoughts and experiences, so that they are modelling responsibility for themselves and their own actions.
- provide opportunities for their adolescents to talk about what is happening for them in daily living (without being invasive)
- communicate from a place of 'I' rather than 'you'.

Teenagers want to belong

A sense of belonging is a fundamental need of all human beings. We all want to belong – to a parent, a family, a classroom, a school, a partner, a neighbourhood, a country. The drive to belong with others, particularly in childhood, reflects an attempt to find safety to be yourself in the outer world. The ultimate goal of maturity is to belong to yourself in a conscious, open and fearless manner; this conscious belonging to yourself provides an inner stronghold that enables you to live your life with a sense of peace, ease and security. Belonging to yourself does not mean living a life of isolation; on the contrary it is this inner stronghold that enables us to reach out to and engage with others without fear. The journey towards conscious belonging to yourself is only beginning for teenagers, and social safety is crucial for them to proceed on this journey. The process is made easier for teenagers when the holding worlds they experience convey clearly to them that their presence is valued and their absence is noticed and matters.

In their drive to belong, many individuals feel demeaned and wounded because of relationships characterised by an over-belonging or an under-belonging, with some feeling utterly abandoned because of a sense of no belonging at all. These relationships can occur not just in the family but also, and very significantly, in the school holding world. *Over-belonging* refers to the kind of relationship where everything is done for the son or daughter by a parent, and where any attempt by the young person to challenge this lessening of individuality results in emotional rejection. This kind of relationship is created defensively by parents who, because of their own inner insecurity, have an overwhelming need to be needed and who become threatened by any displays of independence on the part of the teenager. *Under-belonging* refers to the kind of relationship where a parent has a very strong defence of wanting to be in control and the children dare not challenge that control. This family holding world is characterised by dominance and high demands for conformity to the 'shoulds' and 'have tos' of the dominating parent. If the young person were to attempt to challenge this controlling parent, she would risk the social and emotional peril of being exiled. Most children in such a situation will, wisely, conform and live their lives according to the demands and commands of the leader of the family environment; they know unconsciously that it is too dangerous to do the real thing of living their own lives and conformity is a clever substitute that keeps them at least somewhat safe. Some children will choose rebellion as their unconscious substitute; attempting to force the significant members of the family to do for them what is too dangerous for them to do openly themselves, that is let them live their own lives.

No belonging refers to the very dark kind of relating where the child experiences anonymity or major violation of her sacred presence. Despair is likely to arise here unless the young person manages to find very powerful substitutes – such as drugs, alcohol, violence, profound dependence and helplessness, or serious illness. In a family where no belonging exists, the teenager unconsciously knows the dangers of reaching out for love and recognition. Tremendously safe holding would need to be created in order to entice the adolescent who has been so wounded to emerge from the shadows of addictive or other powerful protective responses. As long as the substitute responses serve the purpose of maintaining some sense of fullness, they creatively will be held on to; however, were the substitute responses to lose that power, then the ultimate protective behaviour may be employed – suicide. Suicide is often about a person ending the pain of having no safe place to be oneself.

When the need to belong is responded to in a real and open way, such that teenagers feel unconditionally seen for their unique and individual presence, then it becomes safe to be themselves.

CHAPTER THREE

'Whose life am I living?' A key question for parents

- Parents' quest to be real
- Substitute responses that reflect confusion
- Substitute responses that reflect crystallisation
- Substitute responses that reflect a sense of invisibility
- Real responses that reflect a strong sense of self
- Mining substitute responses for the diamond of the real self

Parents' quest to be real

In order for parents to support and guide their teenage children effectively in coming into possession of themselves, parents need to have to come to a resolution regarding their own sense of self (this, and all that follows in this chapter, also applies to teachers and other significant adults in the lives of teenagers).

When parents are stuck in a confused or crystallised sense of self, or lack any sense of self, it is likely that their sons and daughters will struggle greatly with expressing their own individuality. Teenagers need their parents to have the inner stronghold of a solid sense of self, a sense of their own separateness and independence; an inner stronghold from which they can operate confidently and maturely. But the reality is that most parents struggle with occupying their own individuality. The most crucial parenting responsibility is for each parent to resolve his or her uncertainty about him or her self. It is only when parents can consciously govern themselves that they truly are ready to head a family. In any society, parenting is the most important profession and, yet, there are no requirements, or systematic supports or provisions, regarding training and preparation for the complex role of rearing children. Safe holding for teenagers in the wider holding world of society requires that, as a society, we acknowledge and support the profession of parenthood. When parents are not in a position to take on the responsibility of self-possession, great suffering can emerge from their unresolved quest for realness.

Those parents who have a confused sense of self are revealing their deep fear of being authentic, real, spontaneous and true to their own individuality. Clearly, they have not found in their adult holding worlds the unconditional holding and support that would enable them to reveal that which during their own childhoods they had had to hide – their true nature – from their parents and other significant adults. No parent wants to stay in a state of confusion and uncertainty, but the suffering that arises from such a poor sense of self pales in comparison to the suffering experienced from the harsh rejection that they experienced in their earlier lives; a suffering they are terrified of re-experiencing. An underlying terror of showing your uniqueness and individuality is also exhibited by parents with a crystallised sense of self and, even more profoundly so, by those parents who feel invisible.

Parents who have found the emotional safety to begin the process of strengthening their sense of self, need to identify the wise and ingenious defences they have created to screen their true self; they need to get under those substitute responses and uncover the hidden expressions of self that need to be brought to light – physical, emotional, sexual, intellectual, social, behavioural, creative and spiritual. This process is aptly described by a phrase used by Deepak Chopra – 'mining the diamond'. Most of all, parents need the love, support and encouragement to love themselves unconditionally in the same way that they want to love their children. Love for themselves is the surest route for parents to provide the unconditionally loving holding that their children need and deserve. This is what it means to say that all parenting starts with the self.

Substitute responses that reflect confusion

Parents who have a confused sense of self may manifest their inner turmoil in any of the following ways:

- by being aggressive
- by being impatient
- by being irritable

- by being controlling
- by being dominating
- by being dependent
- by being manipulative
- by being indecisive
- by being anxious
- by being cynical
- by being unreliable
- by being irresponsible
- by avoiding risk taking.

All of the above responses are unconsciously created, substitute means by which parents seek to protect their individual wholeness. These substitute responses are created in childhood to stave off the pain of the absence of unconditional holding and the threats to spontaneous expression of their unique nature. Unless parents seek out the safety that will enable them to move from the substitute ways to real ways of holding their wholeness, their defensive responses not only mean that they stay hidden but also they will pose considerable threats to the wellbeing of their teenage children. When parents are too frightened to reach out for help for themselves to resolve their abandonment experiences, it behoves the other significant adults in teenagers' lives to challenge and support – compassionately, but firmly – these parents to seek resolution of their confused state. It helps enormously when these significant people create an unconditional and empowering relationship with teenagers in the family who may be, themselves, in inner turmoil. Of course, there is no guarantee that other adults in teenagers' lives are any more mature than the parents and they also may not notice teenagers' inner distress.

The level of confusion varies from mild to severe; one measure of severity is the number of the above substitute responses that are used. The frequency, intensity and duration over time of these substitute responses also provide a measure of the level of inner confusion.

When a parent fails to recognise any of the above listed responses as part of his behavioural repertoire, there is a strong possibility that he is in denial. Denial is itself a powerful defensive strategy and one that is very worrying as teenagers can be at great risk in the face of such defensive blindness. Teenagers with such parents require some mature adult who will validate their experiences in regard to their parents, who will recognise the threats they are encountering daily, and who will respond with the kind of loving holding that gives hope to the teenagers that the confusion of the parents will not be repeated in the young people.

Substitute responses that reflect crystallisation

Crystallisation refers to the situation where a parent has over-identified with one of his own parents and lives out the life of that parent rather than his own individual life. These parents have not cut the umbilical cord; emotionally and socially they have not flown their original family nest and they remain strongly enmeshed with one or both parents. Such entanglement with their own parents leads to a repeat of the entanglement with their children. 'Lean-to-relationship' describes the relationship these parents have with their teenagers; the expectation of the parents is that the teenager will conform to the ways of the parents, and woe betide him if he should protest. Some substitute responses typical of parents who are entrapped in a crystallised sense of self are to be:

- conformist
- over-involved with family of origin
- timid around their own parents
- neglectful of their present family in favour of family of origin
- dependent
- invasive
- over-demanding
- addicted to what others think
- fearful of change
- perfectionist
- depressed
- driven
- over-pleasing
- compliant
- sensitive regarding family image.

Here again, some indicators of the depth of crystallisation are the frequency, intensity and persistence over time of the substitute responses.

The challenge with parents who operate from a crystallised sense of self is that they can often appear to create the perfect family, but the reality is that, within themselves, there is a deep level of conflict arising from the sad fact that they have not lived their own lives and do not occupy the house of their own individuality. To allow such conflict to rise to consciousness would mean risking a recurrence of the rejection experienced in earlier life and so they keep any thoughts of liberation firmly repressed. It is not unusual for these parents to experience deep depression in their middle age, a wise and creative strategy that attempts to draw attention to what lies hidden – the 'diamond' of their own true self.

The emphasis on 'family' rather than on each person's individuality within the family and the pressure to maintain a strong family image militate against the mature development of teenage children, and of the parents themselves. Conformity to parental ways is what is expected and it would be emotionally perilous for teenagers to go against the family grain. Within this family, teenage turmoil is highly likely to go undetected as its recognition would threaten the 'perfect image' of this apparently successful family.

Substitute responses that reflect a sense of invisibility

Because of unspeakable violations during childhood, there are parents who wisely have buried very deeply any open expression of their true nature. These parents will declare that they feel invisible, worthless, 'a nothing', ugly, unlovable; they complain of feelings of emptiness, isolation, overwhelming depression, shame and terror. In order to stave off a recurrence of the early experiences of annihilation, they have creatively extinguished the light of their individuality. It takes a very powerful, consistent, unconditional relationship to entice them out of the darkness they inhabit daily. These parents need professional psychotherapeutic help because, otherwise, they will remain steeped in their misery and pose great threat to the wellbeing of their children. Because of the severity of the violations experienced, the substitute responses developed have had to be equally severe in nature, and include the following:
- being addicted to alcohol
- being addicted to drugs (prescribed or illegal)
- being addicted to food

- being addicted to work
- being addicted to sex
- being violent in relationships
- being extremely passive
- being tremendously shy
- being hypersensitive to criticism
- being deeply pessimistic
- being highly critical of themselves
- being highly critical of others
- engaging in self-harming.

These kinds of substitute responses reveal the dark inner void that needs to be filled; when the substitute behaviours cease to work in covering over the void, attempted or actual suicide is often the final protective endeavour – the underlying meaning is that 'at least when I'm dead, I don't have to continue to experience the absolute misery of invisibility and the experience of not being loved for myself in this world'.

Vigilance on the part of significant adults other than parents is vital for the children of parents who hate themselves. The tragedy is that the adult associates of these parents often occupy a similar dark inner world. In this situation, there is a very important role for safe holding of teenagers in environments outside the family by, for example, neighbours, teachers and members of the clergy. Often, teenagers who live in these homes, because they are so deeply troubled and troubling, can encounter further rejection in their schools and communities and so the whole sad cycle of invisibility recurs in their young lives.

Real responses that reflect a strong sense of self

No parent escapes from bringing at least some inner conflict from his childhood, but there is a small minority of parents who do have a strong sense of their individuality and who mostly reside in the home of their own unique self. These parents, from an interiority of light, relate maturely with their children in a way that is of an unconditionally loving and empowering nature.

The real responses that are characteristic of parents who have largely resolved the question 'Whose Life Am I Living?' include:

- being unconditionally loving

- being independent
- being able to communicate directly and clearly
- being honest
- being understanding
- being encouraging
- being respectful
- being non-conformist
- being empathic
- being supportive
- being affirming
- being accepting
- being responsible for themselves
- being empowering.

Teenagers, who are fortunate enough to have had, from early childhood, parents who are emotionally secure and confident, have the advantage that the seeds for them finding their own selves have been sown since conception. These teenagers will have experienced unconditional love, a belief in their immense ability, and will have been given age-appropriate opportunities to actualise their potential. Because the parents themselves inhabit their own individuality, their teenagers will be affirmed and supported in their individuality and in their particular ways of expressing themselves within the family. These teenagers will also have encountered very definite boundaries in regard to their parents' responsibilities and their own responsibilities. Mature parents do not allow their children to slide out of responsibility, and where there is conflict boundaries will be maintained (see Chapter 7). Mature parents will spot if the behaviour of their teenage child is suggesting some inner distress, arising, for example, from bullying in school, needing more preparation to take on new challenges or because of conflict with a teacher (see Chapter 10).

Mining substitute responses for the diamond of the real self

Parents with a confused or crystallised sense of self, or who feel invisible, are faced with the challenge of providing the mature parenting of themselves that their own parents were not able to offer. The past cannot be changed, but the substitute responses that were created can be brought into consciousness and understood, and then new choices and actions can be taken. Every adult is faced with the responsibility for giving full expression to their individuality and true nature. When parents are not in a secure place to take on this responsibility, everybody suffers – most of all themselves but also their children. The journey towards the mature parenting of the self is unique for each person; each parent will have developed a unique set of substitute responses in reaction to the defensive responses of their own parents. It is good practice for parents to begin to identify and take note of their present substitute ways but it is crucial to hold on to the realisation that these responses are creative and that, without them, they would not have survived their own childhood abandonment experiences.

The great wisdom in the substitute behaviours created is that the opposite of what is exhibited is the real response that has had to be hidden and that now needs to be expressed. The substitute behaviours provide the window into what is crying out for resolution; when the behaviours are held in compassion and explored for their loving message, then the diamond of truth, of realness, begins to shine forth. But this is not an easy exploration as it involves mining through layers of defences built up unconsciously from the early years of life. The innate wisdom of the child buries feelings of abandonment and also creates defences in response to the hurts experienced – it means that the child does not consciously have to endure pain on a daily basis.

Listed in the tables below, under the different kinds of protective sense of self, are examples of typical substitute responses and their opposites that signify the underlying hidden, real responses that need to emerge. It can be seen from the lists that if real responses were the common way of interacting, life would be very different for both parents and teenagers. But, of course, if it was easy to respond in a real way, this is just what parents would do. The truth is that for parents who have been deeply hurt in their own childhoods there will be great fear and reluctance to now do what they dared not do when they were children. The challenge is that the 'enemy' is still out there – in the sense of others' defensive behaviours – and their new mature ways may well be ridiculed, rubbished and rejected by their own parents, or by brothers, sisters, friends or workmates. Rocking the family foundations may very well spark off powerful reactions in those who, in their own defensiveness, supported the dark edifice of conformity. Finding support and making friends with others who are also seeking emancipation helps hugely with staying on the road to maturity. Parents may also find support in the knowledge that staying on the mature track will be of enormous help to their teenage children in finding their maturity. Parents can be assured that when they find a solid sense of self and begin to act maturely with their teenage children, they will experience a lifetime of a deepening relationship with them, based on separateness and independence rather than on conformity and dependence.

TABLE 3.1: CONFUSED SENSE OF SELF: SUBSTITUTE RESPONSES AND OPPOSITE REAL RESPONSES

Substitute response	Real response
being aggressive	being assertive
being impatient	being patient
being irritable	being calm
being controlling	being self-controlling
being dominating	being in charge of self
being dependent	being independent
being manipulative	being upfront
being anxious	being secure
being cynical	being direct and clear
being unreliable	being reliable
being irresponsible	being responsible
being avoidant of risk taking	being a risk-taker

TABLE 3.2: CRYSTALLISED SENSE OF SELF: SUBSTITUTE RESPONSES AND OPPOSITE REAL RESPONSES

Substitute response	being over-pleasing
being conformist	Real response
being enmeshed	being authentic
being dependent	being separate

Substitute response contd	Real response contd
being invasive	being independent
being disappointed	being respectful of privacy
being over-demanding	being empathic
being addicted to what others think	being responsible
being fearful of change	being affirmative
being perfectionist	being welcoming of change
being depressed	being realistic
being driven	being optimistic
being ambitious	being authentic
being compliant	being assertive

TABLE 3.3: FEELING INVISIBLE: SUBSTITUTE RESPONSES AND OPPOSITE REAL RESPONSES

Substitute responses	Real responses
being addicted to drugs (prescribed, legal or illegal)	filling the void with the nectar of love
being addicted to food	being nurturing of yourself
being addicted to work	working on an unconditional relationship with the self
being violent in relationships	being kind in relationships
being extremely passive	being strongly assertive
being tremendously shy	being spontaneous
being hypersensitive to criticism	being separate from what others say
being deeply pessimistic	being highly realistic
being highly critical of yourself	being affirmative of yourself
being highly critical of others	being encouraging in relationships
engaging in self-harming	engaging tender with yourself

Parents who occupy the dark interior world of feeling invisible are, not surprisingly, slow to trust others; it is for that reason, and their unconscious terror of further experiences of harsh abandonment, that they are often very reluctant to seek professional help. Furthermore, because their substitute responses are of such an immensely powerful nature, and because of the threat they pose to themselves or others, the response they most often receive is not understanding but medication; a response which only serves to depersonalise them further. Whilst medication may be of some benefit in reducing symptoms, it does nothing to bring forward the hidden self of these highly troubled and troubling parents. Resolution is slow and comes about with a psycho-social practitioner who can create relational depth, understand the wisdom of the distressing responses, feel compassion, and provide the belief and support required for all that lies hidden to gradually emerge.

CHAPTER FOUR

The importance of parents parenting themselves

- All parenting starts with the self
- Parents being responsible for their own needs
- How parents parent themselves: The impact on teenagers
- The challenge of parents' challenging behaviours

All parenting starts with the self

All adults have a responsibility to resolve the emotional and other abandonments they have experienced in their earlier lives; when this responsibility is not followed through, they continue to suffer greatly – but so, too, do others who are exposed to their defensive responses.

Adults who become parents have an extra responsibility on their shoulders to come into maturity so that they can become 'good-enough' parents. In parenting, actions speak louder than words and so parents need to be sure that what they expect from their children is what their children witness in their parents' behaviour. For example, a parent who does everything for her children but expects and does little or nothing for herself is utterly confusing for young people; the lack of congruence between how she relates to herself and how she relates to others creates insecurity. Similarly, if a father complains that he is 'breaking his back' working for the family but shows no great effort in caring for himself, then he is displaying contradictory behaviour that serves only to induce fear in his children. Parents have a duty to parent themselves in all the ways that they would want to parent their children. Sadly, many parents struggle with the notion that all parenting starts with the self. As seen in Chapter 3, such mature parenting is unlikely to emerge when parents still have a sense of their own self that is confused or crystallised, or when they experience themselves as being invisible. Parents who possess a strong sense of their self have little difficulty in grasping the truth that all parenting starts with the self.

Each of us knows in our core how to be loving; problems arise when the nature of our holding worlds leads us to a defensive disconnection from our core being. Parents do not need to be taught how to love, but they do need very definite supports and guidance to rise to the challenge of finding a resolution of their own insecurities so that their true nature may shine forth in their relationships with their children. In an ideal world, parents would spontaneously offer the necessary safe holdings to their children, but the reality is that parents come into their child-rearing role with their own emotional vulnerabilities because of the lack of, or inconsistent, holdings in their own childhoods. In our work with families and individuals, it is possible to trace the origins of distress and turmoil back five, six, seven generations. No parent wants to block the mature development of her children, but parents can only bring children to the same level of development that they have reached themselves.

The most common defensive position of parents is either to 'be there' too much for teenagers and not there for themselves, or to try to make the young people 'be there' for the parents and not there for themselves. There is also a tragic minority of parents whose presence has been so darkened that they do not permit even a glimmer of their true selves to appear. These parents, who are so alienated from themselves, neither give to, nor expect to receive from, their children. Their lifestyle reflects their interior blackness: drop-out from all challenges, apathy, hopelessness, despair, aggression, violence, addictions to alcohol, drugs or work, lovelessness, isolation, and neglect of their physical and emotional welfare. Clearly, the level of support and guidance required is much greater for the latter group in resolving their inner turmoil.

Just as for teenagers, parents too have a deep need to belong, but that need may not have been safely held; their experience of belonging may have been one of over-belonging, under-belonging or no belonging. Whatever their experience has been, parents bring that experience to their children and, unless they have at least gone some way towards resolving any belonging issues they may have, they will not be able to provide for their children the safe holding that nurtures a true sense of belonging.

The particular kind of parenting that each parent needs to provide for herself can be discovered by her exploring her sense of self and the substitute behaviours she may have developed in the face of unsafe holding (see Chapter 3). In effect, parents now need to be father and mother to themselves, in all the ways that their parents were not because of their vulnerabilities. Parents need to engage in a relationship with themselves that has the qualities of unconditional love, nurturing, respect, support, tenderness, kindness, belief, understanding, encouragement and independence – all the qualities that they would wish to offer in their relationships with their children. In practice, a loving relationship with themselves has a myriad of faces, including being affirming of themselves, taking good care of their physical selves, listening to their own inner voice, identifying their needs, being in touch with and valuing all emotions, and, where necessary, talking out their emotions in openness from a place of ownership. The care of yourself also involves rest, time for reflection, responding from a place of spontaneity and authenticity, and taking control of your own life.

It is not too difficult to detect the different kinds of troubled relationship with oneself that can exist among parents, nor is it too difficult to create opportunities for change in the sad circumstances of troubled lives. But, sadly, the emotional, social and spiritual wellbeing of people has not been a priority in our culture because it entails all of us examining our inner and outer lives. Until we create the safe holding in all our social systems for individuals to own, express and seek resolution of their self-doubts, conflicts and vulnerabilities, it will continue to be difficult for parents to parent themselves.

Parents being responsible for their own needs

A competition of needs arises in all relationships, between parents and children, lover and lover, friend and friend, husband and wife, employer and employee; a crucial dimension of mature relating is that each person in the relationship takes ownership of and responsibility for his or her own needs. It can be quite a challenge to respond to needs in this mature way. Take the example of the parent who, in evident exasperation, exclaimed, 'My children are driving me wild, can you help me?' The response from the therapist was, 'Sure; the first thing that strikes me is that it is not your children who are driving you wild, it is yourself.' When asked, 'What are your needs?' the parent responded with 'peace and quiet'! 'A very legitimate need,' the therapist responded, 'but your children miss you all day and they probably want a wild time with you when they see you.' In the therapeutic relationship, the father came to see that his children's needs were just as legitimate as his and that responsibility for his need for 'peace and quiet' lay with him and not with his children. He recognised that, certainly, he could make requests of the children or negotiate a mutual meeting of needs but, ultimately, the responsibility of meeting his own needs rested with him.

Parents 'passing the buck' of responsibility for their needs onto their children is a common source of conflict between parents and children. Another example of a parent passing the buck of responsibility for her needs onto her child involves a young woman on a bus with a toddler in her arms. At one point, the toddler started pulling his mother's hair which, from her facial expression, was causing a considerable amount of pain. She put up with it for a time and then suddenly 'played dead'. She did it well, to the extent that panic crossed the toddler's face that he had killed his mother. Without realising it, this young mother was making the child responsible for her pain and this was probably not the first experience for the child of getting the strong message that he was responsible for his mother's needs. What could the young mother have done in the situation? She could have gently but firmly taken the child's hands from her hair and declared, 'I don't want you to do that; it hurts.' By taking responsibility for her own pain, she does not blame the child, does not frighten the child into conforming, and she sends out a clear message around her boundaries of care for her own physical wellbeing. She also models for her child how he can take responsibility for his own needs.

A not uncommon message – often unspoken but yet powerful – within homes is: 'For peace sake, don't upset your mother (father).' Similar proscriptions can operate within other holding worlds, such as schools, churches, workplaces and sports clubs: 'Don't upset the teacher'; 'Don't upset the priest'; 'Don't upset the boss'; 'Don't upset the manager.' What, then, are people to do with their own upset? The word 'upset' is typically understood to mean 'distress', but a much more powerful understanding is that the 'set-up' (up-set) needs to be 'turned over' as it is seriously making it difficult for the individuals concerned to be honest about their needs and grievances. It is much easier – for children and adults alike – to take responsibility for their needs when it is safe to do so – safe physically, sexually, emotionally, intellectually and socially. In the case of teenagers, any threats to their sense of lovability make it very risky for them to be there for themselves. In this case, their wise strategy is to conform to the pressure to take on responsibility for their parents' (and other adults') needs and to suspend their own needs – particularly those needs that the adults in their lives are not in a mature place to meet. In the case of parents, it is imperative that they free themselves of what was 'put upon' them as children and begin to be true to themselves, express and take responsibility for their own needs in relationships, and refrain from taking responsibility for the needs of others. The danger is that when such freedom is not attained they, in turn, will pass on their emotional defensive strategies to their children and the whole sad saga will repeat itself.

The aspect of responsibility with which most parents struggle is *to take ownership of* their own responses. Out of a fear of being strongly there for themselves, they can project responsibility for their feelings, words and action onto their teenagers:

- 'you made me angry'
- 'you deserved what I said'
- 'you drove me to hit you'
- 'you make me so mad because you never listen'
- 'you only think about yourself'
- 'you're making a laughing stock of me'
- 'you're disgracing the family'
- 'you make me ashamed to be seen in public with you'
- 'you let me down'.

In examining the above responses, what stands out is the absence of the 'I'. It is of note that the central letter in the word respons-*i*-bility is 'I'; the presence of 'I' demands that parents take ownership of their own responses and any actions that such ownership calls forth. Take the example given above of 'you made me angry'; responsibility here requires the 'I' message, 'I feel angry' and requires the parent to figure out what actions she is being directed to take for herself. Anger is an energy from the self to mobilise the parent in response to some unmet need or unexpressed value or belief. When the parent blames the teenager, she is looking to the teenager to take responsibility for her unmet need, but the parent is 100 per cent responsible for her own needs.

Like 'passing the buck', 'taking the buck'– whereby the person takes responsibility for the feelings, actions and needs of another – is another aspect of the struggle parents can experience around having mature responsibility for themselves. When a parent takes on total responsibility for her children's needs, she effectively deprives them of opportunities to learn to be responsible for themselves. Again, the parent who takes the world of the family on her shoulders does so unconsciously and, unless challenged in a non-threatening way, will continue to do so. The origins of 'taking the buck' of responsibility lie in her childhood where to gain recognition and reduce the threat of being hurt, she wisely learned to be the 'good girl' who minds everyone, but who, sadly, neglects herself. Turning this around to being responsible for herself is no easy task, but it is an urgent task in the move towards maturity. When no change occurs, this parent creates a great deal of helplessness in her children as the children wisely understand that to allow themselves to need the parent is the safest option in the face of her defensive need to be needed.

If parents had the good fortune to be reared in an environment where they were given daily opportunities to learn to take responsibility for themselves, then they would automatically own and take action around their own needs, beliefs and values. But, if parents have not had such early safe holding, is it any wonder that, as parents themselves, they act in ways that are in keeping with that early holding?

It is a much harder challenge to learn responsibility for yourself as an adult. Nevertheless, the responsibility lies with the adults – if they are safe to do so – to ensure that children live in environments where being responsible for yourself is central to family, community and school wellbeing. Those parents who do not have the psycho-social readiness to create mature relationships with their children, need to urgently seek help to redress the situation – a critical act of responsibility.

How parents parent themselves: The impact on teenagers

There is no doubt about it – how parents relate to their own selves directly influences how they relate to their children. The degree of intimacy that a parent has with herself is the degree of intimacy she will have with her teenagers. When such intimacy is lacking, in spite of a parent's best intentions, it will adversely affect her relationship with her children. If she does not know herself, how can her children know her? If she is not in tune with her own feelings and needs, how can she be in tune with the feelings and needs of her children? If she is afraid to be herself, how can she allow her children to be openly and freely true to themselves? It can be a major challenge for parents to take on board the responsibility of having a loving relationship with themselves; this is understandable in holding worlds – for example, church and society – that do not encourage love for yourself, but instead brand such love as 'selfish'. When there is a 'community' of people making the journey inwards, the responsibility of parents to love themselves can be carried much more easily.

In considering their relationship with themselves, it is useful for parents to explore how safe or threatened they feel in regard to the different expressions of the self:

- physical
- sexual
- emotional
- intellectual
- social
- spiritual.

For example, when parents physically nurture themselves, keep themselves fit and healthy, eat, drink and party in responsible ways, and enjoy and enhance their appearance without being obsessed with it, then they provide a model of authentic physical self-expression for their teenagers. If, on the contrary, a parent treats her body like a workhorse or she is preoccupied with her weight and diet, or she frequently criticises or expresses hate of her body, how can she inspire her adolescent children to treat their sacred bodies with love, care, respect and nurturing? Should a parent discover that she relates unlovingly to her physical presence, it is very important that she seeks help and support to understand what has brought her to such a dark place, and to learn how to uphold her physical integrity. Given the ever-increasing focus on 'the body beautiful' and consequent protective responses among young people – such as anorexia nervosa and bulimia – the need is urgent for parents to find authentic physical self-expression for themselves.

With regard to sexual self-expression, the general picture emerging from national and international research is that young people tend to look to other sources – such as friends, school and the media – rather than to their parents for information on sexuality-related matters (see Hyde et al., 2009). Sadly, many people have experienced unsafe holding around sexual self-expression, ranging from abusive experiences to the more everyday proscriptions and prescriptions that typically surround us. In response to unsafe holding, parents may find themselves with sexual hang-ups, they may find themselves homophobic, embarrassed around the topic of sexuality and frightened of or 'turned-off' by sexual expression. Such substitute responses are urgently calling for attention to the hidden truth that needs to emerge – sexuality is an integral aspect of our human nature and, as such, deserves to be openly enjoyed and celebrated. When the truth does not emerge, not only is there great loss for the parents but also for their sons and daughters who intuitively pick up on their parents' inner conflict around this aspect of self-expression.

In terms of emotional self-expression, parents need to ask themselves the following questions:

- To what degree do I internally feel the warmth of unconditional love for myself?
- Am I comfortable in the giving and receiving of love with another?
- Do I value *all* feelings and take due action *for myself* when necessary?
- Am I comfortable when family members express emergency and welfare feelings and do I facilitate them in responding to their feelings?

When parents have difficulty in the internal expression of love for themselves, this, naturally, will impact hugely on their children. Given that the cause of most human problems is a lack of loving, it is urgent that such parents get help to resolve their own losses and consequent repressions. There are some parents who can shower affection on others, particularly children, but have grave difficulties in receiving love. Their 'shower of love' is not real because it carries the condition that the child must accept it or risk the possibility of rejection; this parent cannot allow the child to refuse, because that is the condition she has set for her worth. This one-sided love creates emotional enmeshment that is very difficult to unravel when the children come into adult age. There are parents, too, who are not able to show affection and whose home-life consists of rules and regulations, rather than loving relating. Such an emotional desert has grave consequences for the wellbeing of children, as they pick up that their presence matters less than that things are done properly. It is important also for parents to be open to the full gamut of emotions available to us as human beings and to respond to emotions as our most powerful barometer of our wellbeing; welfare feelings, indicating a state of wellness, and emergency feelings, signalling a threat to our wellness.

Parents can help enormously in nurturing authentic intellectual self-expression in their teenagers when they believe in their own immense intelligence and do not confuse knowledge, or performance or educational achievements, with their innate intelligence. As there are few adults who know their innate genius, why should it surprise us that the majority of adolescents appear to go for the average (an ingenious way of offsetting the threats that come from the identification with failure or success!). Both experiences have become the greatest impediments to young people's progress. Parents need to redeem their sense of their own limitless intelligence and get back to the adventure of learning that was so present when they were toddlers.

The development of relationships outside the family can be a hugely challenging experience for adolescents. Social self-expression can be an area of particular vulnerability for teenagers and enormous hurts can be endured, sometimes with tragic consequences. Young people need parents who enjoy relationships outside the family and who are sure of themselves in different social settings. Parents who are socially insecure, shy, timid or aggressive and loud in social situations are not able to provide a safe social holding for their teenagers; these parents deserve to be given opportunities to develop their own social confidence and competence.

In regard to parents having a sense of our nature being spirit, at present, in Ireland the holding world of society is in the throes of a secular revolution and many parents, and other adults, are struggling with finding a spiritual meaning to life. In many ways, coming out of a history of religious conformity, it can be more difficult for Irish people to discover the spiritual dimension of being. There is evidence from research done by Eckersley (1995) in the US that having a sense of connectedness to something that transcends the material world and its addictions to success, wealth and status, helps young people because it provides an alternative perspective when the going gets rough. Ultimately, we all need to make our own spiritual discoveries, but for teenagers it is supportive when the parents themselves convey a sense of recognising, honouring and valuing the integral spiritual dimension of our human lives.

The challenge of parents' challenging behaviours

One of the realities of family life is that both parents bring their own emotional vulnerabilities into their parenting role. Nobody escapes having some doubts about their worth and capability but, clearly, the level of vulnerability ranges on a continuum from low to extremely high. The origins of inner conflicts are not genetic in nature, but emotional vulnerability does get passed on from generation to generation unless, somewhere along that generation line, parents stop, reflect and take the necessary action to bring about maturity in their own lives. As already noted, it is not that parents ever want to interrupt the wellbeing of their children, but the reality is that this is what happens when they have not resolved their own inner emotional and outer social conflicts.

The outward manifestations of a parent's inner emotional vulnerability become the challenging behaviours that threaten the wellbeing of teenagers. Challenging behaviour is best defined as those actions or omissions that, whilst they invite the parent to reflect on his or her inner turmoil, pose a block to a teenager's mature development. Take, for example, a father who is addicted to work, has high expectations of himself and others and is short-tempered. His frequent absence can lead his teenage children to feel that his work is far more important in his life than their presence. The father's unrealistic expectation of high academic achievement undermines his teenagers' sense of their lovability and capability and, in their defence, the teenagers, cleverly, may either become work addicted and a perfectionist like Dad or totally react against his way of doing things. The teenager who reacts goes the opposite to her father's ways and so, for instance, she will hate and avoid schoolwork and be utterly careless in the way she carries out tasks. The father's short-temper poses a threat to the teenagers expressing their feelings, thoughts, unmet needs and grievances. Some of the teenagers may develop the defensive behaviour of passivity, while others may rebel against the father's short-temper and become even more aggressive than the father himself. Whether passivity or aggression ensues, the sad cycle of the father's emotional vulnerability begins to be repeated in his teenagers' lives.

What does maturity require of the father in this example? He needs to recognise his challenging behaviours, see the effects his responses are having on himself, his wife and his children, and be determined to resolve his inner emotional conflicts. This is a big undertaking which can only be taken on in an environment of non-judgement, understanding and compassion. If he finds he is not resolving his inner conflicts, it is crucial that he seeks out professional help for the sake of himself, his marriage and his children. It is an act of caring and courage to be able to face into one's defensiveness and seek the appropriate psycho-social help necessary to make mature progress. The deeper the level of maturity of a parent, the more he or she has to offer in terms of the wellbeing of the family.

A challenging behaviour more typical of mothers is being over-involved with their children, not allowing them to do things for themselves, thereby inducing in the children the challenging behaviour of helplessness around the care of themselves. Where there is an over-belonging, maturity requires of the mother that she reflect on the extent to which she belongs to herself; it is only in the resolution of this that she will be in a position to give and receive care in relationships and provide the opportunities for her children to learn to take responsibility for themselves.

Teenagers can experience many challenging behaviours from their parents – irritability, anxiety, over-protection, aggression, unrealistic expectations, ridicule, disappointment, scolding, addictions, depression and passivity to name but a few. It is crucial that parents reflect on what makes them act in these ways towards their teenagers and that they take ownership of their responses and refrain from blaming (another challenging behaviour) their teenagers for their responses. All actions, words, thoughts and feelings on the part of parents are revelations about the parents and are not caused by teenagers or others. When parents own their responses, reflect on them and take the corrective actions needed, the world becomes a safer place for everyone, but, most of all, for children and teenagers.

CHAPTER FIVE

Some key dimensions of the parenting of teenagers

- Teenagers' views on their parents' parenting
- The need for democratic parenting
- The need for parents to know their teenagers
- The need for empowering parenting practices
  - *Enabling teenagers*
  - *Supporting curiosity*
  - *Belief is everything*
  - *Appreciating difference*
  - *Teenagers' 'freedom to party'*

Teenagers' views on their parents' parenting

A 2004 survey of 500 13–18-year-olds in Britain carried out by *Reader's Digest* found that teenagers rated mothers above fathers in all but one of the 36 categories of parenting investigated; these categories included communication, advice giving, school homework, listening, sexuality, public outings and privacy (Readers Digest, 2004). The exception was driving and one has to wonder why that was ever included in the survey as an important parenting category! The survey raises serious questions about the high number of teenagers who not only rated fathers as being poor at parenting, but also their mothers. For example, whilst it appears positive that 59 per cent of young people give their mothers an A (excellent) or a B (pretty good) on the sensitive parenting skill of advice giving, it has to be acknowledged that for 41 per cent their experience was less than good. On this particular parenting skill, only 35 per cent of fathers scored an A or a B, which leaves a large majority of 65 per cent of teenagers unhappy with paternal guidance. On the crucial communication skill of listening, 73 per cent of mothers gained an A or a B, while only 53 per cent of fathers gained such high grades.

Whilst a worrying result for fathers, it comes as no surprise that mothers were rated higher than fathers across all the meaningful parenting categories; sadly – for both the fathers and their children – the father is still the 'forgotten parent' in many ways. Being without a strong fatherly presence is likely to make it particularly difficult for male teenagers to find their way in answering the question of how they want to be in the world. In order for teenagers to progress towards maturity, they need safe holding from both their parents. There needs to be exploration of the threats that exist for men that make it difficult for them to take their full place in parenting, and opportunities and supports need to be provided that will enable men to find the safety to be present, involved and real in their relationships with their children. Mothers suffer too when fathers are not fully engaged in joint parenting. In contemporary society, mothers too tend to have their own careers but still carry the major share of parenting responsibilities; an imbalance that carries health risks for the women concerned.

A worrying outcome of the 2004 survey is that 43 per cent of the adolescents surveyed felt that they could manipulate their mothers while one-third felt they could manipulate their fathers. It is often because of the weakening of parental resolve that teenagers get themselves into trouble. Parents require considerable help and support to maintain appropriate limits and to know when it is appropriate to relax those restrictions (see Chapter 7).

It is interesting that on 'letting teenagers be' – which is about their right to physical and mental privacy – fathers scored higher than mothers for the age range 15 to 18 years. Given that fathers generally are less involved than mothers in parenting, one wonders whether this outcome has less to do with parenting skills than with the level of non-involvement by fathers, which may lead to them asking less intrusive questions or being less likely to barge into their teenager's private space. Adolescents' private thoughts deserve respect, their rooms are their castles, not to be invaded without invitation or raided when not there. Although they may not show it, adolescents need their parents to trust them. When a parent has a doubt, it is best to talk directly to the young person and not go behind his back.

All the indications from the survey are that a greater drive is required not only to enhance the parenting skills of both mothers and fathers but to create a greater degree of joint parenting and a greater level of co-operation between parents. The typical family set-up puts quite a burden on mothers who need more support and encouragement to voice strongly their need for their male partners to share the exciting and often challenging task of parenting children. Fathers, too, need support to voice their need to take their rightful place as making a difference in their children's lives.

The need for democratic parenting

The kind of understanding that parents have of what parenting is about is a crucial influence on how effective they will be in guiding their children's development and the consequent level of responsibility the children will show in their teenage years. Many parents still view parenting as a matter of controlling their children into doing what they see as being right for them. Children appear to be resisting this type of parenting, but it is of concern that, increasingly, such children are being brought to child-guidance centres and counsellors' rooms by despairing parents. Children dare to do today what their parents would never have thought to do in their relationships with their parents.

The challenge of rebellion has emerged from general cultural changes that have taken, and continue to take, place. Intuitively children and teenagers sense the democratic atmosphere in the wider holding world of society and are much more likely to hold on to their dignity in the face of their parents' and other adults' attempts at authority over them. When teenagers assert their right to say no to a request and the parent retaliates with, 'You'll do as I tell you', a vicious cycle can develop in which the parents attempt to hold their stance of control and the teenagers 'dig in their heels' and absolutely refuse to be dominated or coerced. In such a conflict situation, attempts to subdue the teenager are mostly futile, as teenagers can be far more resilient than adults in holding on to their resisting stance. Furthermore, most teenagers are not inhibited by social consequences, by 'appearances' and are free of the time constraints under which parents typically have to work. Sadly, because there is defensiveness on both sides – coming from fear and self-doubt – the home can become a battlefield where there is little co-operation and no harmony but instead there is hostility, frustration and a feeling of helplessness on the part of the besieged parties.

Anytime parents order a teenager to do something, or try to 'make him do it', they invite conflict. This does not mean that parents cannot guide or influence their teenagers into responsible behaviour, but it does mean that parents need to find a different and more effective approach. Parents – as well as teachers and other significant adults – need to let go of their defensive authoritarian ways and assume a mature approach that is respectful and effective. It is important that adults realise that though the old dominating strategy may have been effective in bringing about compliance, it was not effective in raising teenagers' self-esteem or in teaching them self-control and mature self-responsibility. Indeed, the old strategy induced fear, low self-esteem and helplessness in many teenagers.

Many parents will claim defensively that they are being 'firm' when they are being controlling and that they are acting for 'the child's own good!' Some ways for parents to check whether they are being maturely firm or defensively controlling are given below:

- Is the parent's own prestige involved?
- Does the parent want others to see what an obedient teenager he has?
- Does the parent have a sense of satisfaction when the teenager complies?
- Does the parent desperately want to be known as a 'good' parent?
- Does the parent want to feel he has the 'upper hand'?
- Does the parent feel that the teenager 'should' obey?

Another way for parents to assess their 'good' intentions is to reflect on what follows the particular interaction with a son or daughter: does the young person continue the same difficult behaviour in spite of the parent's attempts to gain compliance? Does he exhibit defiance? Does the parent feel angry, resentful and even more determined to gain control? It is important also for parents to notice the message being conveyed through their body language; for example, stiff body posture, arms folded across the chest, fire in the eyes, and a tone of voice that is commanding, aggressive, insistent and demanding. Mature intentions will be reflected in relaxed body posture and a quietly firm tone of voice.

The word 'authority' is best interpreted by parents as 'authorship of self'. Parents – and other adults – need to accept that they simply do not have authority – in the sense of control – over their children. Young people know this even while adults struggle to accept it. Parents can no longer demand, control and impose and need instead to practise 'authorship of self' whereby they are firm about the action they will take for themselves, rather than focusing on what they are going to make the teenager do.

The parent, as leader, needs to assess the demands of the situation and work towards fulfilling those demands, not just his own preference. Understanding, listening, encouragement, logical consequences, mutual respect, respect for order, co-operation, all come into play in the quest for harmony. Above all, parents need to be vigilant about how they are acting in the situation; it is so easy to slip back into being authoritarian. Parents need to constantly remind themselves that: 'I cannot force my teenagers to do anything nor can I forcibly stop them from doing something. I may try all the tricks in the book, but I cannot force my son or daughter into co-operative action.' Mature behaviour needs to be stimulated, brought out in the young person, not commanded. Parents can employ their ingenuity, creativity, tact, patience and sense of humour to promote co-operation.

Democratic parenting is far more challenging and requires more personal reflection and responsibility than parenting by force but the gains of the former approach far outweigh those of the latter – parents feel far more in charge of themselves, their relationships with their teenagers are far more harmonious and their teenagers learn one of the central aspects of maturity – self-control.

The need for parents to know their teenagers

You can know another only to the extent that that person is willing to share his inner world with you. In relationships, having this kind of knowing can be powerful in engendering understanding, compassion, empathy and responsiveness. In the relationship between parent and teenager, it is crucial that the parent creates the safe holding that encourages the teenager to share his inner world. In order to create the necessary safe holding for the teenager, the parent needs to be secure in his own revealing of himself; something that many parents can find quite challenging. Parents can defensively delude themselves that they know their teenage children and can be in quite a state of denial when trouble knocks on the family door – 'I know my son would never do anything like that' – even though the proof of the 'wrongdoing' is staring the parent in the face. This kind of denial can spring from the fear of not being seen as a 'good' parent; the parent who cannot allow that we all get it wrong sometimes will find it very hard to see any 'wrong' in his offspring. Inability on the part of the parent to face how things can be, means that the teenagers of such a parent are likely, in response, to keep secret many aspects of their lives.

Of course, it is not just a question of knowing a teenager in case he might get into trouble – knowing the other is crucial to the overall quality of the relationship – but being able to get to know another starts with a person knowing him or her self. When parents do not know themselves, they are unlikely to have the inner safety to get to know their adolescent son or daughter. The old saying 'if you want to know me, come and live with me' is not always borne out in experience; parents and children can live together and have very little sense of what goes on in each other's lives. Getting to know another takes being interested in the other, engaging in active listening, being non-invasive and having a willingness to self-disclose.

Real knowledge of another can only be gained through the open experiencing of the other; it will never be had through subterfuge which breaks trust in the relationship. Teenagers, rightly, are often very strong on the issues of privacy and needing their own space; their own room is their private space as is a diary containing their private and sacred thoughts on themselves, their relationships, the past, the present and the future. As pointed out in the preceding section, some parents will justify intrusions into a teenager's private space by saying, 'I only did it for your own good.' In their hearts, the adolescents know that the parents were actually serving their own defensive needs and so will resist any further attempts on the parents' part to get into their world. Being 'known' in the relationship is a two-way street between parent and teenager. Parents need to give their children a knowing of their own needs, hopes, fears and expectations in the relationship.

Clearly this is difficult for the parent who has a worry that a son or daughter may be taking drugs, abusing alcohol, engaging prematurely in sexual activities, not being where they are supposed to be or being where it is not safe for them to be. In this case, the most effective approach is for the parent to bring his concerns to the young person, not in any accusatory way, but openly and honestly; for example, communicating 'I am worried that you may be experimenting with drugs and I want you to know that I care for your welfare and am here for you.' The parent needs to watch for the young person's response, particularly the body language that accompanies any verbal attempt to reassure such as, 'Ah, Dad, there's no need to worry about me.' When there is no accompanying eye contact, or the tone of voice is tentative or the message is given 'on the run', then further expressions of concern are required, along with closer but open supervision of the teenager's whereabouts. Whether teenagers like it or not, parents are legally responsible for their welfare up to the age of 18, and in order to fulfil this responsibility, parents have a need to know, for example, whom the teenager is with, where she is going and what time she will be home. When teenagers do not co-operate with these needs of parents, parents are called on to set down very definite boundaries around what is permissible and not permissible, but they need to ensure that their expectations are reasonable, and that they are always respectful in the way they express these needs. In the situation where a teenager is regularly non-co-operative, a deeper knowing is required to find out what is happening for the teenager that stops him from being responsive.

The checklist below is a guide to some of the important things that parents need to know about their teenage children:

- What gives your teenager satisfaction and joy?
- What are your teenager's hopes and dreams?
- What distresses your teenager?
- What are the life questions that engage your teenager?
- What challenges are important to your teenager?
- What are his experiences of and what meanings does he attach to sexuality?
- Who are his friends; do you know their names, where they live, their telephone numbers?
- What are the names of and have you met the parents of your teenager's friends?
- What school subjects does your teenager like and which does he dislike?

- Is your teenager content and challenged in school?
- Which teachers does your teenager speak well of and who are those he resents? Do you know why?
- Is your teenager interested in any sport? Does he have any favourite sporting team/figure?
- What kind of music does your teenager listen to most? Who are his favourite singers, groups or composers?
- When troubled, to whom is your teenager most likely to go?
- If your teenager drives, do you know that he drives responsibly, in a way that is conscious of his own safety and that of others?
- Is your teenager passive or aggressive? Do you know what has given rise to and presently triggers these responses?
- Is your teenager interested in reading? What books or magazines does your teenager read most?
- Is your teenager interested in film? What is your teenager's favourite type of film?
- Is your teenager interested in computer games?
- How much time does your teenager spend watching TV? How much time does he spend on the computer?
- What does your teenager most love to do in his spare time?
- If your teenager has a part-time job, have you met the employer?

If parents have the answers to the above questions, this indicates a strong knowledge of their teenagers; not having any of the answers sounds the alarm on the need for the parents to find the safety to create the kind of relating that leads to knowing on both sides.

The need for empowering parenting practices

It has been seen in previous chapters that unconditional love is the deepest longing of teenagers – as it is for all of us – and the efforts parents make to respond to this need are the bedrock of effective parenting. Whilst unconditional love is the bedrock, there are certain specific practices that are essential to the mature parenting of teenagers; some of the most important are the empowering practices that help the young person to reach two of the primary goals of adolescence – independence and self-responsibility.

Enabling teenagers

Parents need to understand that coming into a sense of their own power is one of the major challenges of the teenage years. This, of course, is also a major challenge for many adults as Nelson Mandela – quoting a Marianne Williamson poem – noted in his 1994 inauguration speech: 'Our deepest fear is that we are powerful beyond measure.' Being powerful can be threatening in holding worlds where the significant adults – particularly parents and teachers – are either 'over-powering' in their ways of relating or are modelling under-use of their own power ('under-powering)'. The teenager who learns through harsh experience that 'my parent has all the power here; he has the power to wipe me out if he wants', will wisely develop protective strategies, such as passivity, hesitancy, wariness and conformity, and will learn to bow to the power of others.

There is another kind of relating that also makes it dangerous for the young person to be in his own power and that is where the parent – out of his own defensive need – does everything for the child. Young people in this situation know instinctively that it is safer to take on the mantle of helplessness than to assert their own power to look after themselves; they learn to give away their power to others. It can be seen that *under-powering* and *over-powering* are two sides of the same coin of powerlessness. The parent who relates from an inner stronghold knows that the power we have is *not power over another* but instead the *power to strongly take our wellbeing into our own hands.*

There are many practical ways by which parents can support and enable empowerment in teenagers – as the examples below show – but the most important support that parents can provide is that they themselves take up the challenge of being powerful and model mature, committed, persistent and active care of themselves:

- provide age-appropriate opportunities outside and inside the home to practise independence (from childhood)
- show belief in their undoubted capacity to take on responsibilities
- encourage responsible use of pocket money (budgeting, saving, etc.)
- allow them to express their own opinions and discuss differences that will inevitably arise
- encourage and support their own decision making

- give responsibility for particular domestic tasks (do not reward chores; chores are an intrinsic aspect of family life)
- ask their opinions on the challenges that you are facing yourself.

Supporting curiosity

During a visit to an art gallery in Toronto, Canada, in an area devoted to introducing children to the joy and excitement of painting, we were very taken with some of the sayings displayed around the walls:

- 'Inside each one of us is an artist and that's what an artist is – a child who has never lost the joys of looking at life with curiosity and wonder.'
- 'To paint without curiosity and to live without seeking is to stop growing.'
- 'The outstanding quality that a teacher must have is absolute belief in the power of the child to live his own way.'
- 'There is no right or wrong way to paint.'

It is said that knowledge is power and, clearly, young people need knowledge in order to be powerful in taking charge of their own wellbeing; they need to be safe to learn, in the ways encapsulated in the above sayings. It is not possible for parents – or other significant adults – to inspire young people to retain their eagerness to learn and their unique ways of being if they have suppressed these qualities in themselves. All sorts of hurtful experiences may have led parents to lose their curiosity and wonder – for example, not being believed in, lack of encouragement, humiliation, harsh criticism, impatience, comparisons, aggression, labelling as 'slow', 'weak', 'average', pressure to perform and unhealthy competitiveness; the frequency, intensity and duration of these defensive responses also has a telling effect on the degree of loss experienced. Unless parents recognise the fears engendered in themselves by their early hurtful experiences and unless they find empathy and compassion for themselves in their fears and hurt, then the sad cycle will keep repeating.

As well as avoiding the kind of hurtful experiences in the examples above, parents need to:

- encourage exploration and experimentation in their children
- encourage young people to see that 'knowing I don't know is powerful'

- affirm for young people that they have everything they need to learn about and manage their worlds
- encourage them to move from outside judgements of 'right' and 'wrong' and instead to check against their own experience
- support them in being open to experiences of 'failure' and to see 'failure' and 'success' as equal partners in the process of learning.

Belief is everything

Recently, in a therapy session, a young man burst out with passion, 'Tony, belief is everything', and, of course, he is right. Belief is the affirming of the other person's limitless capacity to take charge of his own life. The complete belief in and support of teenagers' capacity to 'live their own way' is essential to their sense of being powerful in their lives. Teenagers possess an endless capacity to learn and to express themselves in their own unique ways. Each teenager brings a giftedness and vast potential to the different holding worlds to which he belongs – primarily home, school and community. It is for adults to spot and nurture these qualities through showing belief in the teenager. Parents show wisdom when they recognise the individuality of each child in the family; any attempt to treat all the children in the family as the same fails to show the absolute belief each child requires. The absence of affirmation of the young person's power to live his own way is a major block to his coming into maturity. Affirmation of this power to live their own lives does not mean giving teenagers licence to do whatever they like; on the contrary, young people need to be shown that real power, as opposed to 'over-powering', carries responsibilities towards their own self and others. Again, parents can only provide these opportunities for young people when they have retained the belief in themselves to live their own ways but, sadly, such confidence is not common because our holding worlds do not often support it.

Appreciating difference

An important way in which parents can enable the young person to be powerful in living his own way is to acknowledge and appreciate the differences among siblings. All members of the family have the unconscious drive to find their own particular ways of expressing their individuality and this needs to be openly encouraged by the parents. Each family member develops personal qualities and a repertoire of interests and behaviours that can be very different from a brother or sister. Different family members also develop their own particular protective strategies; take, for example, the twin boys described by relations as 'chalk and cheese' – if one was the rogue, the other was the serious child; if one was street-wise, the other was street naive; if one was good at looking after family members' needs, the other was good at getting others to look after his; if one was top of the class in school, the other was bottom; if one was a dare-devil, the other was cautious. Of course, parents will also tend to be different in their ways from each other and the child who fits in with one parent's ways – rather than challenging these ways – is more likely to be the favourite of that particular parent.

Birth order can also be an influence on the extent to which different family members have the safety to express their individuality and their power to live their own way. It is often the case that the eldest child in the family is loaded with responsibilities compared with younger siblings and this can lead to displacement onto younger siblings of resentment towards parents for the unfairness of always having to be the 'responsible one'. Such displacement can be expressed in controlling and aggressive responses – *over-powering* – towards the younger members of the family; often persisting into adulthood. Not surprisingly, the younger siblings will, in turn, resent being 'bossed' by their older siblings and this, too, can persist into adulthood. The middle, or 'sandwiched', child in the family can find himself fighting to establish his individuality on two battlefronts with both older and younger siblings. It can happen that this child has to fight more to gain attention and affection but this is determined more by the nature of the relationship each parent has with the middle child rather than by his position in the family.

Parents also need to be careful that male and female family members are given equal opportunities to express their individuality and their power to live their own way. It is not uncommon in families for the girls to be expected to look after the boys and to do most of the domestic chores. It is also not uncommon for girls to be given the message that certain elements of powerfulness – such as decisiveness, active problem-solving, assertiveness and firmness – are not part of femaleness. Likewise, for boys there are certain elements of powerfulness that are not encouraged in them; for example, domestic self-care, such as cooking, laundry and ironing, and attentiveness and responsiveness to emotions.

Some principles of good practice in supporting all family members to be powerful and to live their own way include:

- encouraging and supporting differences in interests, aptitudes, perceptions, experiences and means of self-expression
- creating separate and unique relationships with each child in the family
- creating opportunities for co-operation among family members
- creating opportunities for the open resolution of conflict when it arises
- responding openly and firmly to any manifestations of rivalry among family members
- ensuring a fair sharing of domestic and family responsibilities
- treating sons and daughters as equally deserving of all opportunities for experiencing their power to live their own way
- celebrating each person's particular achievements, joys and satisfactions in life.

Teenagers' freedom to party

Recently, a mother described to us how taken aback she was with her child's exasperated response to a request she had made, 'Mum, I'm only four'; this response alerted the mother to the fact that her expectations were unrealistic and needed to be tailored to the child's age-level. If children have the right to be children, then teenagers have the right to be teenagers – but teenagers' definition of that right may differ markedly from that of their parents, teachers and other adults.

Belonging to a group is an important part of being a teenager and the 'right to party' is an aspect of this need to belong and be accepted by your peer group. When such partying results in drunkenness, destructiveness and riotous behaviour, then 'right' become 'might' – becomes *over-powering* – and cannot be tolerated by adults, who should exercise their power to look after the wellbeing of their teenager. As seen earlier, one of the challenges that teenagers face and struggle with is that parents have legal and moral responsibilities around the wellbeing of young people up to 18 years of age. In her recent book, Clare Healy Walls (2007) defines responsibility as the 'ability to respond' and she makes the useful distinction between being 'responsible for' and being 'responsible to'; pointing out that parents are not directly responsible for their children – the children themselves are responsible – but parents are responsible to help children be responsible for themselves.

In order to become responsible, young people need freedom not 'licence'; when given licence they are not required to take responsibility for their choices but, when given freedom, responsibility is integral to their actions.

When young people fail to exercise the responsibilities inherent in freedom, then the freedom needs to be withdrawn and re-negotiated later when commitment to being responsible is forthcoming from the young person. It is wise for parents to start the responsibility-giving process at the earliest stage by creating opportunities for age-appropriate responsibilities and maintaining firm boundaries. When this process is maintained, teenagers' 'right to party' is accommodated in mature ways, by both the parents and the young person. When such effective parenting has not been present, then teenagers will find it difficult to be maturely powerful and, at times, 'all hell' will break loose.

We have worked with families where children and adolescents were grossly verbally abusive of parents, were destructive of property, and threatened, robbed and lied to get their own way. In such situations, it is the parents who urgently need the help and support to create boundaries around their own responsibilities as parents and to exercise their power to safeguard their own wellbeing.

CHAPTER SIX

Expressing individuality: A key process in the teenage years

- The challenge of 'being yourself'
- Expressing individuality
- The self as creator
- Self-esteem: The reflection of the screen self
- Creating safe holding for the real self to emerge

Expressions of self
- Safe physical holding
- Safe sexual holding
- Safe emotional holding
- Safe intellectual holding
- Safe behavioural holding
- Safe social holding
- Safe creative holding

The challenge of 'being yourself'

The teenager experiencing doubts and fears in facing into a new challenge – for example, a first date, interview for third-level course, making a speech at an end-of-year event marking students' achievements – can often be met with the response from an adult of 'just be yourself'. One wonders whether adults who say that realise precisely what they are saying or, indeed, meaning. One of the most challenging things for adults themselves is to 'be themselves' – to be real – most are quite fearful of truly expressing their beliefs and values, and, most of all, inhabiting their own individuality (see Chapter 3). 'Being yourself' is likely to be a far harder inner challenge for the young person than the outer circumstance she is facing, such as going on a first date.

When, through the early years of infancy and childhood, young people have not experienced the kind of holding from parents, teachers and other significant adults in their lives that was affirming of their unique presence and did not celebrate their intelligence beyond measure, then the truth of who they really are may need to be well and truly hidden. The unconditional love of children provides them with the security that no matter what they do or say, or how they look, or whether they are healthy or ill, they will be seen and loved. The enablement of children provides further security for their true self to emerge. Enablement means affirming the amazing potential of the child to gradually understand and take charge of all the worlds she will encounter, and providing the opportunities for her to discover these worlds through her own experience. When they emerge into the teenage years, children need to have the solid inner foundation of an unshakeable sense of their lovability and individuality and of their power beyond measure. When children reach their teenage years without such an inner stronghold, facing into new challenges – such as entry into second-level school, new peer groups, emerging sexuality, new knowledge fields, greater academic responsibilities, career decisions, developing independence and becoming self-realised – becomes a daunting prospect.

Teenagers who, for example, struggle academically, who are hostile, moody, unco-operative, shy, timid, aggressive, destructive or addicted to substances, will not be able to let go of these substitute responses unless consistent attention is paid to creating the relationship environment that makes it safe for them to be real, to be true to themselves. What is often missed is that those teenagers who are compliant, high achievers, perfectionists, addicted to success, people-pleasing and shy are also acting from a defensive rather than from a real place and, because their flags of distress go unnoticed, they can be more at risk than those teenagers who act out their inner distress. Adults who are themselves not afraid to be real are the ones who notice these different defensive responses from teenagers. If the signs of teenagers' fear to be true to themselves are missed, this signals the need for the adults to reflect on how they feel about themselves.

Parents – indeed any adult who spends significant time with children and teenagers – need to have a knowledge and understanding of the nature of the self and of the shadow world of defences and the screen self we develop in the face of threats, if they are to be able to provide the safety for young people to allow their true self to emerge openly and spontaneously.

Expressing individuality

For the child, the primary process is to attract her parents; this attraction is her security that her parents will be there for her in the way she so badly needs. Parents are the centre of the child's life and so it is from the parents that the child takes all her cues – effectively the child needs to live her parents' life until it becomes safe for her to begin to live her own life. If the parents are solid in themselves, then the child will know that her ability to attract is a given and comes from her unique presence; she will now be safe to be herself. Parents who are mature will make it safe for their child to start taking her cues from herself, to be her own unique self; doing this by showing interest in her, enquiring, checking with her, taking her into account, listening and helping her find her own answers to the questions that turn up in her life. The child in this kind of family holding world will be safe to live her own way – she will be safe to be her unique self. When parents are not in a solid place in themselves, the child unconsciously understands that there is insecurity about her 'attractability' and she now has to work at finding some way of 'living alongside', of 'fitting with' her parents. Her 'struggle' may take the form either of conformity to the parents' ways or reaction against them; either way the child's focus is completely on the parents as there is too great a threat in being connected in with herself – she cannot afford to be her individual self, she has to live her parents' life.

With the coming of the teenage years, expressing one's individuality becomes a primary focus. In adolescence, a question that comes to the forefront is: 'Whose life am I living?' The impetus at this stage is to start becoming your own person, to live life according to your own lights rather than having an eye to others, to live life from the inside out rather than the outside in, to inhabit one's individuality. This, of course, is a lifelong process but its initiation is one of the major challenges of the teenage years. The teenager who from childhood was encouraged to be her own person will find this challenge much easier to accommodate but it will still be a challenge because she is moving out into wider holding worlds and, very likely, will encounter threats to being herself in these wider worlds. For example, the holding world of peers is very important for teenagers, but peers are very often not in the solid place in themselves that encourages individuality; instead the likelihood is that there will be pressure in this holding world to conform to peers' way of living – pressure to be 'like us'.

The teenager brought up in an unsafe family – and school and neighbourhood – holding world, who already feels unsure about being herself, will find the process of becoming her own person highly challenging. Having learned from early on that she has to keep her eye on the cues coming from others, it is very difficult for her to start checking with herself:

- How do I experience this?
- What's my sense of what's happening here?
- How do I feel about this?
- What's my 'take' on this?
- What does my experience tell me?
- What sits well with me?
- What have I discovered for myself?
- What's my answer to this dilemma?
- What gives me a leap of joy?
- What gives me a sinking feeling?

Teenagers who are already insecure about checking in with themselves may find themselves casting about for guides on how to be in the world – they may, for example, 'try on' the lives of a sporting hero or a favourite pop star or celebrity or an admired teacher or uncle or aunt – or they may stay with their tried and tested defence of conformity to their parents' ways of being in the world.

The self as creator

What do we mean by the self when we use phrases such as 'finding your self', 'self-possession' or 'being your self'? The concept of the self is given a central place in many psychological models of human functioning (for example, Jungian psychology, Psychosynthesis, Core Process Psychotherapy); with variations in the definition of the term and different emphases on different aspects of the self across the different models. In this book, when speaking of the self, we are emphasising:

- the self as unique presence
- the self as 'knower', 'seer', 'witness'
- the self as 'wholeness', as perfect being
- the self as 'creator', as 'executor'.

Intuitively, we can have a sense of ourselves as being unique, as being unlike any other; a distinctiveness that cannot be pinned down to anything tangible, such as a particular physical characteristic, a particular type of creativity, a particular way of relating or a particular way of behaving. This sense of distinctiveness is one of the meanings of self, referring to the fact that I am an unique presence in the world, with my own particular circumstances, my own particular way of looking out on the world, my own unique story, my own way of making sense of the world and my own sense of where I'm headed in life. This uniqueness has a physical manifestation in my DNA; my self is unrepeatable. Intuitively, we also have a sense of something that remains constant in all the passing play of life; for example, my feelings come and go and there is an 'I' that notices the comings and goings, sometimes my behaviour is passive and sometimes assertive and there is an 'I' that notices these different behavioural expressions. This constant 'noticer' is another important dimension of what is meant here by the self. The self is the 'knower', 'seer', 'witness' of everything that turns up in my life.

Clearly, the 'seer', is separate from what is seen, the 'knower' is separate from what is known and the 'witness' is separate from what is witnessed. The self in its separateness is undiminished, unblemished, untarnished by whatever pain, hurt, suffering, abuse or neglect turns up in my life, and, conversely, it is not 'made greater' by any achievements, successes or approval from others that may occur. This untouchable wholeness, rightness, goodness, lovability is a further important dimension of what is meant by the self.

Intuitively, we can also have a sense of ourselves as always 'figuring things out', of making our way through whatever circumstances our lives present us with; this sense of being a 'manager' in our lives is another important dimension of what is meant by the self.

In enabling young people to move towards maturity, it is important for the adults in their holding worlds to understand that, as human beings, we are never victims of what life throws up for us but instead we are creators – always actively creating our own particular responses to the various worlds we encounter (see Humphreys and Ruddle, 2010 for a more detailed discussion of this view). This creative responsiveness is a central aspect of what is meant in this book by the term 'the self'. The self is vastly intelligent and always wise and knows exactly how things are for us at all times; this being true from the moment we come into the world. The infant understands intuitively, albeit at an unconscious level, the extent to which unconditional love is present in the central relationships in her life – the relationships with her father and her mother. When threats emerge in these relationships – for example, lack of responsiveness to her physical needs, coldness in the way she is held, harsh handling, lack of affection, comparisons, lack of welcome for her presence, lack of engagement with her – this causes tremendous pain and her self will find ways of protecting against this pain; for example, using the protectors of being 'demanding', of being 'sickly' or of being very quiet. These protectors, or substitute behaviours, are created out of love; the motivation being to reduce current suffering, to offset the possibility of further occurrences of threat and to call attention to the fact that suffering is present – in the hope that some adult will pick up the distress flag being flown – and to gain some attention, even if of a substitute rather than real nature. The central core of us, the self, is love, and the impetus of the self is always to maintain wholeness, to protect our wellbeing and to try to restore the place of unconditional love.

Self-esteem: The reflection of the screen self

The self cannot be damaged or taken from us; the self is always present with all its wonderful capacity for self-expression, but for many people the self has to keep itself hidden behind protective walls. It is important that the significant adults in the lives of young people understand that safety in the relationships we experience, from childhood through to adulthood, is the crucial context for open, spontaneous, real and authentic expression of the self. From the start of life, young people know in their core about their unconditional worthiness of visibility and love, but if, in their earlier relationships, their open, real expressions are not met with love, then the self recognises this dangerous state of affairs and creates substitute means of attracting some level of attention and some semblance of love. The substitute means that the self wisely creates in circumstances of threat make up what we refer to as the *screen self*. While the screen self is a very wise creation, if the individual lives from this self for the most part, then her life is severely constricted. The challenge for adults in relationship with young people lies not in tackling the substitute behaviours but in getting underneath them so that the young people may be enabled to bring into the light what they are signalling as having had to be hidden; the critical process is one of emerging rather than changing.

The screen self then can be seen as a protective crust a person forms around his or her real self in order to survive in threatening holding worlds. The greater the threats to the real expression of oneself, the greater the protectors needed and the stronger the screen developed. Self-esteem – how one feels about oneself – is best understood as a reflection of the distance between a person's screen self and their real self; where the distance is great, self-esteem will be low and where the distance is small or minimal, then self-esteem will be high.

Parents need to be aware of and alert to the signs of low self-esteem; some of which are not immediately obvious.

TABLE 6.1: CHARACTERISTICS OF HIGH SELF-ESTEEM: LITTLE DISTANCE BETWEEN REAL AND SCREEN SELVES

Natural curiosity
Eagerness to learn
Love of challenge
Emotionally expressive
Emotionally receptive
Adventuresome
Spontaneous
Able to focus on the here and now
Competitive with yourself, not with others
Acceptance of mistakes and failures as opportunities for learning
Fearless
Acceptance of success as a step towards further learning
Listening without interruption
Willingness to listen to feedback
Enjoyment of academic effort
Co-operative

TABLE 6.2: CHARACTERISTICS OF MIDDLE/LOW SELF-ESTEEM: MODERATE TO LARGE GAP BETWEEN SCREEN AND REAL SELVES

Loss of natural curiosity
Physical and emotional withdrawal or physical and emotional clinging
Fear of failure and mistakes
Use of avoidance protectors (apathy, low motivation, poor or no application to studies, non-listening, day-dreaming)
Use of compensation protectors (perfectionism, academic intensity, long hours of study, addiction to success, over-serious, boastful)
Hypersensitivity to criticism
Over-pleasing or rebellious
Shy, or over-compliant or disruptive behaviour, loudness, destructiveness, bullying
Avoidance of challenge or, on the other hand, reckless risk-taking
Competitiveness with others or 'couldn't care less' attitude
Critical self-labelling (for example, 'I'm no good at reading'; 'I'm useless at sports'; 'I'm hopeless at mathematics'; 'Nobody likes me')
Open hostility or silent resentment in response to correction or reasonable demands for more responsible behaviour
Over involvement in sports or other activities
Unco-operative
Blaming of others for own mistakes or feelings
Aggressive or passive
Destructive of own or others' belongings

Creating safe holding for the real self to emerge

In their work with teenagers, adults often speak about raising the young person's self-esteem. A more accurate way of viewing what is needed in the adult-teenager relationship is that the adults, in their behaviour towards the young people, mirror for them their real self – their uniqueness, worth and lovability – and encourage and support them to give expression to their self in their own individual ways – in this book we use the term 'safe holding' to refer to this kind of relating. When teenagers are safe to be real and safe to be their own individual self, then they do not need to resort to the creation of a screen world. Safety needs to be established not only for teenagers to express their uniqueness but to bring forward the fullness of the self across the range of human expressiveness; this range being described below.

Expressions of the self

In our human existence, the self, and the loving energy of the self, is expressed in many extraordinary and wonderfully creative ways through the human capacities available to each and every one of us:

- physically
- emotionally
- socially
- intellectually
- behaviourally
- sexually
- creatively.

The above are means of expression available to the self, but while the self has these wonderful resources, it is not identifiable with any one of them. Assagioli, the founder of Psychosynthesis, puts it like this: 'I have a body but I'm not my body'; 'I have feelings but I'm not my feelings.' This can be extended to all the expressions of the self. The self is the manager or executor of these expressions, and the self knows when there can be open expression and when protective expression is the safest, and therefore the most loving, option. These different forms of expression are the means by which the self seeks to make its presence known, to show its loving nature and to attract love.

It is particularly important for children that the adults around them understand that the self is separate from these expressions and that they are not loved for particular expressions but for themselves; for example, children need to know that they are loved not because they achieve high marks in examination results, or because they are very pleasing socially, or are very well-behaved, or because they are very affectionate, but because of their unique presence. When the person becomes identified with any one of these resources, she is no longer free in her expression – her resourcefulness becomes a means to an end. For example, when a teenage girl becomes identified with her body – 'I have a beautiful body, therefore I must be an attractive person', or 'I have an ugly body, therefore I must be an unattractive person' – then she can no longer just enjoy and appreciate her unique physical presence in the world; she is lost to the truth that she is powerfully attractive in her living presence and her physical expression has become a substitute means of finding her worth. These different expressions are here for the loving purposes of the self, for its real, authentic visibility in the world; they are not here to impress others, to mind others or protect others.

The effort for parents is to do their best to create the kind of relationships that will allow their teenagers to be fearless in giving open, authentic expression to each of these amazing aspects of their being. (Guidance on how to provide such safety is provided in the following sections.) The creation of safe holding for these different expressions of the self among teenagers is only possible when parents, teachers and other significant adults live out their lives from a solid interior world. Adults can bring teenagers only to the level of maturity that they themselves have reached. Adults spill the beans all the time on the level of their own self-esteem – protective responses, such as impatience, perfectionism, irritability, violence, ridicule, scolding, preaching, advising, controlling, dominating, passivity, over-protection and manipulation, all mirror an interior darkness, a screen self that is crying out for resolution. Unless the significant adults in young people's lives resolve their own vulnerabilities, not only are they not in a position to provide the necessary safe holding that elevates the young people's self-esteem, but their defensive responses continue to create threat and resultant misery in teenagers' lives. Whatever happened in the early lives of these adults, the matter is now in their hands.

Safe physical holding

- Parents need to show that they understand that: 'I have a body but I'm not my body', so that their children can also bring home this truth to themselves.
- In early life, the baby's needs are to be held, to be warm, to be safe from any physical threat, to be fed, for thirst to be quenched, to digest, to move, to touch, to explore, to draw attention, to urinate, to defecate and, later on, to feed self, to walk, to risk-take, to take charge of her own bodily functions, to check out her physical world. When the infant's physical needs are met with loving kindness, then that safe holding makes it possible for the child to continue without hindrance to give expression to all her bodily needs. Any impatience,

roughness, ignoring, slapping, shouting, irritability or aggression around any aspect of the child's physical expression will lead to the self repressing the particular expression that was punished. Clearly, the frequency and severity of the parent's – or childminder's or other adults' – responses will have a telling effect.

- Parents need to encourage their teenagers to appreciate and enjoy their bodies for their uniqueness and to relate to their bodies with friendliness and loving care and with appreciation for how their bodies serve them so well in living in the world and their bodies do this irrespective of size, shape, colour or weight (this theme is elaborated on in Chapter 8).

- Parents need to understand that how a teenager feels about her body will have its roots in very early childhood and the nature of the physical holding she received at that time. The teenager who from childhood has experienced affectionate, loving, caring, respectful physical handling, who has experienced physical affection, will find it easier to give real expression to her physical presence.

- Parents need to celebrate with their teenagers whatever physical changes are occurring for them.

- Apart from physical care needs, from their first days in the world, children need to be free from physical judgements – 'she's such a pudgy little one' – and physical comparisons – 'she's much less active than her sister was at that age'. Judgements and comparisons – even when appearing favourable – pose great threat.

Safe sexual holding

Safe holding for sexual self-expression is considered in greater detail in Chapter 8; the following are some of the key issues involved.

- Parents need to understand for themselves and for their teenagers that: 'I have sexual energy but I am not my sexuality.'

- My sexuality is an inherent aspect of my nature and is not defined by sexual activity.

- Parents need to provide, from childhood onwards, age-appropriate information and guidance that will enable their teenagers to stay safe. Ignorance is not bliss when it comes to sexual safety. Neither must ignorance be confused with innocence; innocence means freedom from guilt which comes from openness.

- Openness and celebration are the key responses required so that sexual expression does not become sexual repression.
- Parents need to establish a pattern of talking openly about sexuality and they need to reflect on their own level of comfort with this mode of self-expression.
- Parents need to be alert to the threat of pornography and the degree to which young people can be exposed to this threat.

Safe emotional holding

- Parents need to understand for themselves and for their children that: 'I have feelings but I'm not my feelings.'
- Parents need to create openness to feelings for all members of the family – males and females alike.
- Parents need to be mindful of our fundamental emotional need to be shown love and to know, in turn, that our love matters. Teenagers will have the safety to receive and give love when they experience unconditional relating from their parents.
- Parents need to show that the teenager is loved for her presence; any confusion of her self with any behaviour profoundly threatens her emotional expression.
- Parents need to understand that when there is an absence of unconditional love, the teenager will develop powerful substitutes for the real love she deeply longs for; some of the more common substitutes are food, alcohol, drugs, study, compulsive care of others, sex, power, success and status. If these substitutes are removed, lost or no longer possible, the self may have to resort to more radical creations, such as illness or even death.
- Apart from the giving and receiving of love, the creation of emotional safety also involves encouraging teenagers to identify and respond to the myriad of other feelings we can experience in life.
- Parents need to understand that our feelings are a powerful source of information and they need to support their teenagers in attending to and using this information. Our feelings are always 'right'; feelings let us know exactly our state of wellbeing. Feelings we experience as uncomfortable are just as much our allies as those we experience as pleasant and happy. The former – what we call 'emergency feelings', such as hurt, anger, resentment, terror, despair and guilt – sound the

alarm when our wellbeing is under threat, either from external circumstances or from inner neglect or abandonment of ourselves. Those feelings we experience as comfortable – what we call 'welfare feelings', such as excitement, joy, anticipation, ecstasy and pleasure – let us know that our wellbeing is secure.

- Parents need to model acknowledgement, acceptance and responsiveness towards all of their own feelings and encourage their teenagers to relate to all of their feelings in the same way. The ability to use their feelings to inform their choices, decisions and actions is fundamental to the wellbeing of teenagers, and the modelling of emotional maturity is key to the provision of safety for their emotional expressiveness. The responsibility lies with adults to seek emotional literacy so that they can create emotional safety for young people.

Safe intellectual holding

- Parents need to understand for themselves and for their teenagers that: 'I have intelligence but I'm not my intelligence.' Our intelligence provides the amazing means by which we are able to explore and understand the worlds we have been born into. Safe holding is essential for this adventure to thrive and to be maintained into adulthood. Generally, young children – depending on the nature of the holding in the womb and in early family life – are risk-takers, dare-devils, adventurers, they are naturally curious, love learning and have an eagerness to know, but by the teenage years, very sadly, many of these qualities have gone into hiding.
- Parents need to understand that if open expression of intelligence is repressed in themselves, they cannot create the safety for their children to maintain openness. The first responsibility is for parents to reflect on their comfort with intellectual expression and to become conscious of the threats they may have experienced.
- Parents need to be alert to the many threats there can be – for themselves and for their teenagers – to intellectual self-expression; threats such as impatience, irritability, ridicule, scolding, anxiety, crossness, superiority, helplessness, lack of opportunities to explore potential, lack of interest, comparisons, unrealistic expectations, punishment of failure, over-rewarding of success, lack of belief, and

labelling as, for example, 'slow' or 'genius'.

- Since intellectual safety is absolutely necessary for teenagers to feel 'response-able' and thereby responsible, parents need to strive for the absence of any threats and the presence of belief, encouragement, participation, excitement, fun and the assurance that the unconditionally loving relationship is abiding and does not increase or decrease with achievements or failures in knowledge pursuits. For example, the achievement of a high grade in science deserves to be celebrated but it must be seen for what it is – a reflection of knowledge gained – but never be confused with the teenager's innate intelligence which never has to be proved but taken as a given.
- Parents need to show belief in young people's ability to make sense of what turns up in their worlds and to cope with whatever comes their way. Teenagers need to know from their parents that their intelligence is limitless and that that they have immense power in their own lives.
- Parents need to support, guide and encourage young people to use the power of their intelligence for their wellbeing and to facilitate them in making active choices for themselves.

Safe behavioural holding

- Parents need to understand for themselves and for their teenagers that: 'I engage in behaviour but I'm not my behaviour.' Any confusion of the self with behaviour leads to all sorts of creative protectors – for example, compulsions, obsessions, avoidance, rebelliousness, sickness, fear of failure, addiction to success and manipulation. Teenagers need to know from their parents that their behaviours are their ways of responding to and managing their worlds.
- Parents need to understand that every human behaviour no matter how irritating, troubling or frustrating, makes sense – there is always a psychological 'rightness' to it; this being applicable to parents and young people alike. Unless parents can make sense of human behaviour and show responsiveness rather than judgement, they cannot make progress in terms of resolving behaviours of themselves or their teenagers that threaten the wellbeing of the self and/or others.

- It is important for parents to see that viewing certain behaviours as 'negative' only serves to increase those behaviours because no understanding is shown of why these behaviours are present. The parent who judges behaviour as 'good' or 'bad', 'positive' or 'negative', 'adaptive' or 'maladaptive', 'rational' or 'irrational' misses the wisdom of human responses. No infant emerges from the womb suicidal, vicious, threatening, aggressive, manipulative, passive, shy, obsequious, violent, depressed, anxious or hopeless. It is the quality of the relationship worlds that the person experiences that determines the emergence of such powerful protective responses. These behaviours are not the product of faulty genes, biochemical imbalances or genetic predispositions; these responses arise in relationships, and can be transformed in relationships.

- Parents need to recognise that each child in the family ingeniously develops a repertoire of behaviours that are different to those of brothers or sisters. The purpose is to express in a behavioural way one's individuality. Parents who encourage the child in her particular behavioural expressions are supporting her individuality and unique presence. Any criticisms or comparison, any diminishing or ridiculing of expressed differences creates profound unsafety for the young person to show her true self; she may conform (act-in) and become ever so obedient, pleasing, perfectionist in her behaviour or she may rebel (act-out) and behaviourally find a substitute way of drawing attention to her individuality, or she may develop an illness. Whether a teenager acts-in or acts-out or becomes ill, this is a creative response to the rejection of her behavioural expression of her individuality.

- When teenagers are exhibiting troublesome behaviours, parents need to remember that the teenagers are not out to make life difficult for others, but they are out to draw attention to how difficult life is for them. Essentially, the teenager is desperately asking, 'Is there anybody out there who will see my distress?' – this is the underlying message of every substitute behaviour. Sadly, because of the dark inner terrain of some parents – and other adults in the lives of young people – these cries for help are often unheard. Patience, separateness and the maintenance of the unconditional relationship need to partner the understanding that behaviours, typically seen as troubling or challenging, are more accurately seen as creations that protect in unsafe holding worlds.

- Parents need to help young people to take ownership of their own behaviours, allow them to take responsibility for consequences of their behaviours and support and guide them in managing the consequences.

Safe social holding

- Parents need to understand for themselves and for their teenagers that 'I have relationships with others but I'm not my relationships.' When we do not have a solid sense of ourselves we can become identified with our relationships with others, confuse loneliness with aloneness, and attempt to fill the inner void with constant company. Parents need to understand that living life through others brings co-dependence and is unfulfilling in nature. True belonging involves the loving of the unique being of the other and the receiving of love from that person – no strings attached.
- Teenagers need to know from their parents, and other significant adults, that their presence makes a difference and that when they are absent, they are missed.
- Teenagers, like everyone else, want to belong – to a family, friendship group, classroom, community, church, or sporting or interest group. Teenagers feel disappointment, hurt and abandonment when the belonging experienced is over-involved or under-involved or, even, more seriously, when there is no involvement at all. Unless parents understand that they must first belong to themselves, they cannot relate to their teenagers in the way that fosters true belonging.
- Unconditional valuing of the young person's presence does not mean that parents put up with social interactions that lessen or demean or disrespect their own or others' presence. On the contrary, it involves strong action on the parents' part to assert their dignity but in a way that does not exile the teenager from the relationship. Judgements, controlling or rejecting behaviours on the parents' part will create insecurity for the teenager about her worthiness of belonging. Behaviours such as inclusiveness, warmth, respect, unconditional regard, active listening, equality, tolerance, understanding, empathy, supportiveness and authenticity will foster a sense of true belonging.

Safe creative holding

- Parents need to understand for themselves and for their teenagers that: 'I have creativity but I'm not my creativity.'

- Teenagers need to know from their parents, and other significant adults, that uniqueness is the outstanding characteristic of our human presence in the world; we are each unique in our physical manifestations but also in the different ways in which we give expression to the different aspects of our self.

- Safe holding for creative expression essentially comes from the recognition and celebration of difference. When difference is not appreciated, it will go underground, buried in conformity but still detected in the unique ways that such conformity emerges. Sadly, interruption of creativity through pressure to conform is likely to be experienced by teenagers in all the different holding worlds they inhabit – family, school, community, third-level education and training institutions.

- Parents need to understand that creativity is present in each of us and is not to be identified with a creative product, such as a painting, a piece of music or a piece of furniture. The fact is that our creativity is made manifest each moment in the processes by which we deal with and respond to what arises in our worlds. For example, each teenager in a family will develop her own particular repertoire of behaviours that distinguish her from any siblings; each teenager has her own way of learning; each teenager will have developed the substitute behaviours that encapsulate exactly the aspect of self that it has been unsafe to reveal openly. Creativity is always at play.

- It is important for parents to distinguish between expressions of creativity that come from defensiveness and those that come from openness. Creativity that arises from an open place is not identified with the self by the person – it is not a proof of one's worth. When creativity arises from repression and from the compensatory protective behaviour of having to 'prove' yourself by being, for example, the best mathematician, pianist, footballer, athlete or artist, it is no longer free and unconditional, but is driven by fear. This person will puts all her eggs in one basket and is highly vulnerable to any loss of face. Suicide is a high possibility in such cases. It is often thought that individuals who are creative in a particular field of knowledge – such as music, art, mathematics – are different to the rest of us, 'gifted', but if truth be told, life can often be a constant torment for such individuals.

CHAPTER SEVEN

The importance of boundaries in the parent-teenager relationship

- Boundaries and discipline: Important dimensions of relationship
- The difference between boundaries and defences
- Boundaries are an expression of love
- Punishment is a defensive response
- Fostering responsibility in teenagers
- Parents need to take action for themselves
- True discipline is about safeguarding people's wellbeing

Boundaries and discipline: Important dimensions of relationship

Questions of boundaries and discipline arise in relationships when differences or conflict emerge between the two parties. Whatever the nature of the relationship – parent-child, husband-wife, manager-employee – putting boundaries in place is a fundamental aspect of the mature relationship. Discipline – the protection of the right to wellbeing – is also an issue that arises in all relationships but is an aspect of the parent-child relationship that can acquire particular significance in the teenage years.

The difference between boundaries and discipline is that the former refers to taking action for your own self around your own responsibilities, whereas the latter is about taking safeguarding action in the face of threat to your own or another's dignity and right to wellbeing – action that safeguards the rights not only of those who are threatened but also of the perpetrator of the threats. Boundaries and discipline are a two-way street; the teenager, like the parent, needs to have his boundaries and to be able to safeguard himself in the face of threat from a parent. But it is the parents' responsibility to take the lead and provide the model for the teenager on how to be in relationships in a way that upholds and maintains boundaries, and the dignity and rights, of both parties. Both these dimensions of the parent-teenager relationship are discussed more fully below; parents need to understand what is involved in setting boundaries, how boundaries differ from defences, what discipline involves and how it differs from punishment.

The difference between boundaries and defences

When conflict or differences arise between people in any relationship the more common response of the two parties is defensiveness, but the inevitable result of a defensive response is an escalation of the conflict. As already seen, defensive responses can be categorised as: 'acting-in' and 'acting-out' behaviours, addiction, and embodiment in illness. The aim of these different defensive responses is to avoid facing what is experienced as very fearful – facing what it is within that requires realisation and definite action. The creative purpose of the conflict is to provide the opportunity for those in conflict with one another to examine their own interior worlds and to look at the insecurities and fears they are bringing to the relationship. The examination of your inner world is very challenging, even for adults. For teenagers to begin to engage in such a process, they need to feel very safe in the parental relationship and to have had, from the earliest years, the encouragement and support to check in with themselves (see Chapter 6). When either the parent or the teenager falls into defensive reaction – such as attack, or physical or emotional withdrawal – it is important for the parent to remember that this is not designed to hurt the other; the intention is to stay hidden until the necessary safety has been found to be real and authentic. It is the meeting between the dark interior worlds of individuals that gives rise to defensive reaction, not the relationship between them. As long as the parent or teenager believes that it is the relationship that is the problem, little or no change will occur; it is only change within the individuals that effects enduring change in the relationship. The parent has to take the lead here, and both initiate the necessary changes within himself and also empower the teenager to start his own internal changes.

Parents need to understand that mature resolution of conflict can happen only when the two parties set about having boundaries rather than defences. A boundary calls for an action *for* the self, whereas a defence leads to either an action *against* another or the self. A boundary is the line you draw around your own worth and dignity as a unique human being. It is the '*strong hold*' of self in the face of any threats to your wellbeing, the holding to an inner solidity, from which nobody has the power to demean, lessen or dismiss one's presence. Holding a boundary is about being *proactive* rather than *reactive;* it is about confident responsibility for yourself and for your own actions, and it is about active assertion of your own worth, value, dignity, individuality and sacredness. When conflict arises in the parent-teenager relationship, parents, who have this inner stronghold, will establish boundaries and take definite action for their self in a way that does not threaten the wellbeing of the teenager. An example of a boundary in response to a teenager's refusal to accept a 'no' and his continued attempts to browbeat the parent into giving him what he wants is for the parent not to engage with the threatening verbal behaviour and to go about his own business. It is best if the parent only gives the 'no' response once, and gives an explanation of where his or her 'no' is coming from. If the parent is not secure in himself, the teenager can become adept at breaking down his resolve; which is not good for the wellbeing of either the parent or the teenager. If the teenager resorts to more serious defensive reactions, such as breaking items of household furniture, and continues to do so following a firm parental request to stop, then the parent may need to draw in outside support, such as telephoning the police and reporting the threatening behaviour. The crucial element in establishing a boundary is that the parent takes the action *for* his own self – verbal or behavioural – and follows through on its execution with firmness.

Many parents have difficulty with setting boundaries through definite and consistent action. The resolution of this difficulty is critical to the parents' own wellbeing and the wellbeing of their children; this is particularly so in the case of teenagers who themselves need to find mature ways of asserting their own boundaries.

Boundaries are an expression of love

Because boundaries are concerned with responsibilities, the parents' readiness to set and maintain boundaries is a central aspect of loving parenting practice. It appears that the holding world of contemporary society does not provide much support for either the parents or the teenagers in this aspect of their relationship. A decade ago, in her book, *A Tribe Apart: A Journey into the Heart of American Adolescence*, Patricia Hersch (1999) declared that for teenagers 'the fabric of growing up has been altered'. She believes that today's young people have been left to their own devices by a preoccupied, self-involved and 'hands off' generation of parents. Adolescents, she writes, have been forced to work out their own system of ethics, morals and values, relying on each other for advice on such serious topics as abuse, troubled parents, drugs and sex. There are reasons to believe that in Ireland today some adolescents are faced with this same situation, not because parents do not care, but because they themselves are confused and uncertain about what to believe in and about what boundaries are appropriate. Ireland has swiftly gone from being a singular Catholic to a pluralist society. Whether or not one adheres to Catholicism, it has be acknowledged that the Catholic Church did provide guidance – even if misplaced – on morals, ethics, values and meaning to life. The pity is that the Catholic Church strayed so far from the essential teaching of Christ which is all about love. From a psychological perspective, teenagers thrive in families where parenting is 'hands-on', open, definite and firm. Loving practices, such as the following, typify these families:

- there is a sense of belonging that is unconditional
- parents, while not being rigid, are confident and secure about their responsibilities
- parents model open communication and active and respectful listening so there is safety for all family members to explore their own values, beliefs and experiences and to check in with themselves on what is real and true for them
- parents show their interest in and respect for the experiences of young people that may be different from their own experiences
- parents ensure there is regular, quality family time – meal times, one-to-one times, family outings – that reinforces the sense of being safely and securely held in the family holding world
- parents encourage exploration of and openness to different perspectives
- realistic, age-appropriate responsibilities are set for the young people of the family

- parents spell out what they consider to be fair expectations of themselves of their teenagers and they give an understanding of where these expectations are coming from
- parents make clear what actions they will take for themselves when a boundary has been breached
- parents follow through on the action needed to restore a breached boundary but they do so in a way that does not break the unconditional relationship.

Many parents believe that setting a boundary is all about the behaviour of the teenager whose behaviour is proving challenging. But, on the contrary, a boundary needs to be focused on the parent's own parental responsibility in the face of the teenager's troublesome behaviour. When parents resort to focusing on the teenager's behaviour, inevitably they slip into judging and controlling, which are defensive responses and are always counterproductive. Parents need to remember that the teenager's challenging behaviour is protective in its motivation; it is flagging the teenager's inner insecurities and is not there to annoy or threaten the parent. When the parents are proactive and follow through on their legal and moral parenting responsibility, the conflict is likely to de-escalate quite quickly. A simple example of being proactive rather than reactive is where the parent responds to the teenager's ignoring of a query with the 'I' request, 'I'd like an answer to my question, please.' If the teenager does not reply, the parent goes about his other business and leaves the failure to reply with the teenager. If the parent tries to pull an answer from him he is now taking responsibility for the teenager's responsibility to be courteous, which makes it less likely that the young person will learn to do that for himself. In any case, the query belongs to the parent, and whether or not to answer belongs with the teenager.

Of course, a parent may set a boundary but the teenager may not always adhere to that boundary. Once a parental boundary has been violated, the parent needs to act quickly, calmly, fairly and resolutely to restore his parental responsibility. Such action is an expression of love for all concerned and it creates a secure environment for the teenager.

Punishment is a defensive response

There was a time when punishment was the primary means of educating children on 'right' and 'wrong' behaviour. Parents, teachers and other adults believed they had a right to dominate and have power over children. What is often forgotten is that in the old autocratic society most adults themselves were dominated by people in authority in their holding worlds – for example, by priests, doctors, teachers, social welfare providers and bosses. It is not surprising that dominance as a means of influencing others was replicated by parents in their relationships with their children.

Even though we have moved towards a great realisation of democracy as a way of living together, many of the old punishment strategies persist in the parenting and educating of children. Democracy implies equality and parents and teachers can no longer assume the role of the 'authority' in the way it has traditionally been interpreted – dominance. In a democracy, one individual cannot be allowed to have control over another, whatever the relationship – parent-child, teacher-student, child-child, manager-employee, husband-wife, priest-believer. Dominance – force, over-powering – needs to be replaced with equality, co-operation and respect.

Whether or not adults accept it, children sense – perhaps through their contemporary exposure to the much wider holding worlds brought about by information technology – that they have gained an equal social status with adults; adult power over them is gone and children 'know' it. Adults need to realise the futility of attempting to impose their will on young people. Rarely does physical or emotional punishing – to any degree – bring about lasting submission and, where it does, parents doom their offspring to a life of passivity, fear, timidity and powerlessness, or one of counter-dominance, aggression and rebelliousness.

Confused and bewildered parents and teachers, who have not been trained in democratic ways of rearing and teaching children, may hope that punishment will eventually bring about results, and they defensively blind themselves to the fact that they are actually getting nowhere with their autocratic and punishing methods. At best, force and punishment may produce temporary obedience, but the losses far outweigh the gains – the creation of fear in the young person to be himself, the estranged relationship between adult and teenager, the guilt feelings on the part of the adult who meted out the punishment – wisely alerting him to his own inner conflict – and the missed opportunity to help the child learn self-responsibility.

When it comes to a 'battle' between parents and teenagers, teenagers can be far more resilient and tenacious than adults; they can out-plot, out-manoeuvre and out-last them. Some families in conflict experience from their teenage members a spiralling of rage, aggression, an attitude of 'I can do what I like and you can't stop me' – premature sexual activity, alcohol and drug taking, staying out late, and, sometimes, not coming home until the following day. Attempts by besieged and worried parents to confront the irresponsible actions may be met with aggressive verbal outbursts or violence or storming off or 'silent treatment'. In despair, some of these parents throw up their hands and say, 'I just don't know what to do.' Teenagers know that nobody can force them to do anything – of course, the teenagers equally need to appreciate that they cannot force their parents to do anything. The parents who attempt to force their teenagers to act responsibly pile up more problems for themselves. It makes no sense to correct an out-of-control behaviour with another out-of-control behaviour. Force and aggression only breed force and aggression, and parents, and other adults, have no right to ask teenagers to act responsibly when they themselves employ irresponsible means. What adults often forget is that teenagers learn their punishing methods from adults.

Teenagers need adult leadership, most especially from their parents. An effective leader inspires and stimulates others into actions that suit the demands of the particular challenging situation, and so it needs to be with parents. Teenagers need guidance and they will accept it when they see that they are being treated as equal human beings with equal rights to dignity and self-respect. Parents need to create an atmosphere of mutual respect and consideration that supports the teenagers in being respectful of themselves and others. Of course, no parent wants to act in a punishing manner towards his children, and when he does so, it must be remembered that such behaviour comes from fear and is a defence against inner insecurity and lack of self-belief and self-control. Parents need support to look inward and to see how their outward punishing behaviour of their children is a projection of their own punishing relationship towards themselves.

Fostering responsibility in teenagers

Teenagers do not want to be troublesome; troublesome behaviour always comes from a troubled inner space. In recognition of this, the aim of parents needs to be to create the kind of safe holding that enables natural responsibility to emerge in young people. Parents themselves need to exhibit responsible living on a daily basis if they are to be effective in gaining their teenagers' co-operation. It helps if parents interpret the word 'responsible' as 'response-able' since belief in children's capability is central to their being 'in-control'. Being in control derives from an inner confidence, whereas out-of-control behaviour arises from a person's disconnection from his capability. Ideally, training in responsible living needs to start as soon as children can do things for themselves. Doing everything for children and then suddenly expecting them to be responsible in their teenage years cannot work. Children deserve as many opportunities as possible to actualise their amazing potential to take charge of their own lives. When parents start with the small responsibilities and gradually increase to greater responsibilities, children will continue to act responsibly in their teenage years.

In responding to irresponsible behaviours presented by teenagers it is important that parents take into account the frequency, intensity, duration and endurance over time of the behaviour. Most teenagers experiment and a few excursions into wildness may need to be understood as exploration of areas of experience that have up to now been 'taboo' or restricted. In cases where the battle rages on a daily basis and where, in spite of requests for 'a heart-to-heart' talk about what is going on for the young person, no co-operation occurs, parents need to look seriously at the possibility of seeking outside help.

In fostering responsibility in their teenagers, the first action of parents needs to be reflection on their own behaviours; some of the more fundamental inner queries being:

- Am I *unconditional* in my love of my child?
- Do I communicate *directly* and *clearly*, without any threat being present?
- Do I *request* rather than demand or command?
- (Where there are two parents) Do we *co-operate* in our parenting tasks – as opposed to a false 'united front'?
- Do I talk *with* rather than *to* or *at* my child?

- Do I attempt to *understand* the meaning of the difficult behaviour rather than condemning it outright?
- From a place of love and concern, do I set *definite* boundaries around what is mature and difficult behaviour within the family?
- Am I *consistent* in following through on what I say?
- Do I practise myself the behaviour that I request of my teenager?
- Is stress or marital or family conflict a contributing factor to my teenager's difficult behaviours?
- Are there factors outside the family that may be distressing my child?
- Do I create safe opportunities – such as regular family meetings – where each family member can voice any needs or grievances that may be arising for them?

Parents need to take action for themselves

At times of conflict, it is important that the parent requests to talk *with* the teenager, not *to* or *at*. When parents talk *at* a teenager, they are sermonising, and when they talk *to* the teenager, they are attempting to control; both approaches aggravate the conflict situation because neither the parent nor the teenager is seen. When parents talk *with* the teenager, they make efforts to enrol his co-operation. If the teenager refuses to co-operate, the parents then need to assert the actions they will take; actions always speak louder than words. Those parents who, over the years, have not established strong boundaries around their parental responsibilities may need to seek support from others to be solid and grounded in the face of challenging behaviours that can be presented by teenagers.

If a young person makes an aggressive stand, the parents' actions need to be of a nature that maintains the relationship with the teenager and, at the same time, declares the truth of what it is that the conflict has brought up for resolution. The parents need to openly accept that there is nothing they can do to stop the teenager from doing what he likes, and they need to declare that while they have no intention of being coercive – which would be unworthy of them – that they certainly will not support or collude with aggressive actions. The besieged parent needs to assert, 'I have responsibilities as a parent towards you until you are eighteen years of age, and I intend to carry out these as best I can.' The parents demonstrate that they do not wish to control, or to take action against the teenagers but they will take action *for* themselves.

This 'action-for-self' response will often give rise to the reaction: 'What do you mean you'll take action for yourself?' The parent in this case may make a declaration such as: 'Well, as a parent, I have a legal responsibility, but even more so a loving one, to know where you are, who you are with and what you are doing until you are eighteen! I also have a responsibility to see that you are home at a reasonable time at night, and that you do not break the law against teenage drinking. My preference is that you yourself would take on these responsibilities of courtesy, time-keeping and abstinence from alcohol, so that I am not put in the unpleasant situation of carrying out my parental responsibilities from a position of conflict.' The teenager may attempt to push for details on what actions his parents will take and, sometimes, the knowledge that such actions are a possibility act as a deterrent to the continuation of the challenging behaviours. In the case, for example, of failure to come home at an agreed time, the parents could express the determination to go to wherever the teenager is and, in front of his peers, ask him to come home. If he should refuse, the parent rings the police for back-up to carry out his legal responsibilities. Some parents balk at this saying, 'My teenager would never talk to me again.' This is a threat that no parent can afford to buckle under; to do so would be neglect of self and possibly lead to regret later if the teenager gets into some more serious trouble. In the example of illegal drinking, the parent could go to the pub the teenager frequents, bring his photograph and inform the management that he is underage and is not to be served alcohol. The parent may also need to inform the management that he will take legal action against them if he discovers his teenager is drinking alcohol on the premises.

The purpose of the actions in the above examples is to enable the parents to carry out their parenting responsibilities. Parents who balk at such strong action need seriously to question their boundaries around their care for themselves and their care for their teenage children. Neglect of parental responsibilities is ultimately a lack of loving of both parents and the young people.

True discipline is about safeguarding people's wellbeing

The need for discipline arises when behaviours threaten the welfare and rights of others or the self. Typically, parents see aggressive or 'out-of-control' behaviours as the target of disciplinary practices, but do not appreciate that 'over-controlled' behaviours, such as passivity, are also a source of neglect and need to come under the umbrella of 'ill-disciplined' behaviour. Passivity has resulted in the neglect of many children, teenagers and adults in this country. The 'demonisation' of aggressive behaviours needs to be balanced with the 'de-sanctification' of passivity. In any social system where there are discipline difficulties – home, school or workplace – an anti-passivity campaign is just as necessary as an anti-bullying one. The empowerment of those who are passive (fearful of showing power) is just as important as the empowerment of those who are aggressive and disruptive (which are attempts to over-power). Individuals who are self-possessed and empowered have no need to resort to the defensive behaviours of either aggression or passivity.

One of the many challenges for parents in establishing true discipline is that, in our society, most existing practices are actually abusive in nature, leading to an escalation of problems rather than the desired effect of problem reduction. Parents need support to develop discipline procedures that do not violate the rights of those who display ill-disciplined conduct; any attempt to over-power only reinforces the over-powering aspect of undisciplined behaviour.

The discipline of old, which is still largely practised, was ill-conceived. It was based on the false notion that children (and adults) are fundamentally bad and that the bad should be beaten out of them (by word or deed) and good beaten into them. There are still those who hold that parents have a right to physically chastise children. Violence breeds violence and parents who physically slap children effectively give children permission to use physical force to get their own way in life. With regard to teenagers, central to any effective discipline procedure is acknowledgement of the sacredness of the young person and belief in his fundamental goodness. Certainly, difficult behaviours need to be dealt with, but in a way that does not demean the teenager's presence and does not pose threat to his rights – physical, sexual, intellectual, emotional, behavioural, social, creative and spiritual. When adults, in attempting to discipline difficult behaviours, physically slap, push, shove and pull teenagers, they violate their teenagers' physical rights. When attempts at discipline involves labelling – for example, 'you fool', 'you thickhead' – the teenager's intellectual rights are violated. When feelings are ridiculed or laughed at – for example, 'cry-baby', 'Mammy's little boy', 'weakling' – the teenager's emotional rights are violated. When behaviour is judged as 'bad' or is scorned or ridiculed, the young person's behavioural rights are violated. When a teenager is publicly humiliated, his social rights are violated. It is not true discipline when teenagers who have violated the rights of others get the same treatment in return; this is simply defence meeting defence and no progress can occur in this environment.

True discipline is not about control or punishment, but instead involves the vindication and safeguarding of people's rights and the restoration of any violated rights. Discipline, in the case of adults, lies with those who have been at the receiving end of ill-disciplined behaviour and with the heads of the social system of which they are a member; in the family holding world this is the parent. In the case of young people, they need assistance in vindicating their rights. Certainly, those who have 'lost control', particularly those who persistently offend, need help to discover and resolve the sources of their undisciplined behaviour, but this is a separate issue and must not dilute in any way the actions needed to restore the violated rights of those who have been under threat. For example, if a teenager name-calls his younger brother 'a twit', the parent champions the child by asserting the child's worthiness and asserts *with* the teenager, 'I do not want you to demean your brother in that way, but I do want you to respect him.' Later on, when the child feels that his right to dignity has been restored, the parent can enquire of the teenager, 'I wonder what it was that led you to call your brother that name'? This enquiry is a *beyond* discipline issue and is made with the intention of providing the opportunity for resolution of the hidden issues behind the teenager's outburst.

Discipline needs to be focused on those whose rights have been violated and on the steps needed to restore safety and protection for their rights. The aim of sanctions is to provide sanctuary for those individuals – parents themselves, siblings, peers, teachers, police – whose rights have been violated. One of the most popular sanctions used by parents with teenagers is to declare, 'You're grounded.' However, the 'you' message here makes this a punishment rather than a sanction, and is likely to interrupt the relationship between the parent and the teenager. Certainly, the parent can assert that, 'I'm withdrawing your freedom to be out with friends for a week and I'm doing this in order to manifest how seriously I view the violation and to show how determined I am that each family member's dignity and rights to safety are strongly upheld.' Tone of voice is an important factor in instituting a sanction; an aggressive tone is threatening and punishing in nature, and not expressive of true discipline. The parent needs to maintain his relationship with the teenager, safeguard his dignity and not slip into meeting a violation with a violation.

When true discipline is enacted, resolution of the troubling situation normally occurs – once the dust has settled. When mature efforts at discipline do not bring about the desired effects, then there are deeper relationship issues that need to be addressed.

CHAPTER EIGHT

Teenage sexual self-expression

- Common confusions around sexuality
- A vision for teenage sexual self-expression
- External threats to mature sexual expression for teenagers
  - *Threats from home*
  - *Threats from school*
  - *Threats from peer groups*
  - *Threats from community*
  - *Threats from the Church*
  - *Threats from wider society*
- Internal threats to mature sexual expression for teenagers
- Teenagers' protectors around sexuality
  - *Acting-in*
  - *Acting-out*
- The practice of safe holding for sexuality
- Safe communication around sexual matters
  - *Communication around self-pleasuring*
  - *Communication around sexual expression with another*
  - *Communication around gender orientation*

Common confusions around sexuality

Sexuality is a powerful resource of the self. As with all other resources of the self – physical, behavioural, emotional, social, creative and spiritual – expression of sexuality may be open, real and authentic or it may be defensive. Sexual activity can become a powerful substitute behaviour, especially for teenagers, in the face of threats to a person's sense of lovability and 'attract-ability'. There is much research showing, for example, how teenage girls use sexual behaviour to shore up a fragile sense of self, to prove their attractiveness, and to fit in with their peers (see, for example, Orbach, 2009). Sex can become an addiction in the search for a substitute for the unconditional love that is missing in the person's life. Sex can become a means to an end rather than a joy in its own right. For example, sex can be used to:

- fit in
- be popular
- feel attractive
- feel normal
- get the guy/girl
- avoid being shamed
- show off.

The meanings that parents attach to sexuality have a powerful influence on the level of safe holding that they provide for their teenagers for open and real expression of this dimension of human life. In our work with groups and individuals, the following have emerged as important dimensions of the meaning of sexuality:

- It's a sense of vibrancy; an aliveness; a sense of being in touch with life
- It's some kind of life-force; some kind of essential energy that's integral to life
- It's the ability to experience physical pleasure; the ability to be alive to the pleasures that life can bring
- It has something to do with the power of connection; something to do with attraction between human beings
- It's about feeling really good in my bodily presence in the world and feeling the 'rightness' of that bodily presence
- It's about joy in the physical
- It's about connecting in with another at a deeper level.

Parents, and teenagers themselves, can have the sense that sexuality is something that only begins to arise with adolescence. This view has its source in the confusion of sexuality with physiology. It is true that, in the teenage years, with physiological and hormonal developments, sexual attraction and the possibility of sexual engagement with another come to the forefront, but sexuality is an inherent aspect of our human nature and is present from the start of life. Parents need to understand that the hormonal/physical model of sexuality is not an accurate framework for real, authentic sexual self-expression. Young people need to be shown that there is more involved than knowing the 'mechanics' of sex, that there is more involved than having the physiological wherewithal to perform sexually. Parents need to understand for themselves and for their teenagers that, 'I'm always a sexual being irrespective of my age and whether or not I engage in sexual activity with another.' Teenagers need guidance to at least start the process of understanding the dynamics of sexual aliveness, eroticism, sexual desire, intimacy and meaning. Self-possession is the key to sexual fulfilment but parents need to be mindful that teenagers can be very far from self-possession.

Teenagers can suffer greatly from the *confusion of sexuality with sex*; operating from the view that 'I'm having sex, therefore I must be sexual', puts pressure on young people to find their sense of self through outward behaviours, and deprives them of the choice about if and when they want to engage in sexual activity with another. But choice is crucial in the safe holding of sexual self-expression.

There is another way in which the confusion of sexuality with sex puts pressure on young people and that is that their sense of being sexual becomes dependent on having a sexual partner. Parents need to understand for themselves and for their teenagers that 'my sexuality is a given; it is not something conferred on me by another'. If a teenager believes that it is sexual activity with another that 'proves' her sexuality, then her sense of herself will fluctuate – often wildly – with attraction and rejection from others. In the recent trial of a number of teenagers in regard to the suicide of a fellow-teenager as a result of bullying, one of the young women concerned admitted that she bullied because she lost control of herself when her boyfriend became involved sexually with the teenager who had committed suicide. Teenagers need to know 'my sexuality is always present; it belongs to me; and it is for my joy and pleasure in life'.

Another confusion that wreaks havoc for teenagers – and for adults – is the *confusion of sexuality with outward physical appearance*: 'I'm good-looking, therefore I must be sexually attractive' or 'I'm ugly, therefore nobody could be attracted to me'. One of the major threats for young people in the holding world of contemporary society is the reduction of the person to her outward physical plane and the setting of very definite standards for how that physical plane should look. Even very young children are exposed to and seek to attain these standards and suffer greatly when they perceive themselves as 'not measuring up'. Parents need to understand for themselves and for their teenagers that 'my body is powerfully attractive in itself as a living presence'; 'my attract-ability' is a given and whether or not another responds to that reflects where that other is in herself'. The teenager whose sense of her sexuality is conditional on her outward physical appearance will find it very difficult to find open, real expression of this dimension of life.

A vision for teenage sexual self-expression

In our work with groups and individuals, the vision below has emerged for teenage sexual self-expression. Of course, parents need to be committed to this vision for themselves – and recognise themselves as being worthy of such a vision – if they are to be credible and convincing in holding it up to young people:

- To see sexuality as something beautiful, open, joyous, right
- To be able to celebrate their sexuality
- To be aware of the influences that impinge on them and be able to evaluate those influences maturely
- To be able to make free choices for themselves; to be non-conformist
- To not do anything they do not want to do; to not act out of pressure
- To be able to say no; to be able to set boundaries
- To be able to say yes when that is right for them
- To stay in touch with themselves; use their feelings as their guide; to know what is fitting for them
- To have a solid sense of self; to be able to be his/her own person; to be self-possessed
- To be able to take action for themselves
- To keep themselves safe
- To be able to communicate openly about sexuality
- To be respectful of themselves and of others.

It can be seen from the above that in enabling mature sexual self-expression, enablement of self-possession is the key; it is not *what* the young person does/does not do, it is not *with whom* she does/does not do it, the crucial thing is *who* she brings to it – whether she is acting from her screen or her real self (see Chapter 6).

External threats to mature sexual self-expression for teenagers

Teenagers, in their wisdom, always want the best for themselves and when they behave sexually in ways that jeopardise their own and/or another's wellbeing, parents need to hold consciousness that these troubling behaviours are a defence against threats in their holding worlds – either within or without. External threats can be conveyed in different ways – verbally, behaviourally, through attitudes, through unspoken messages, through the language used, through silences, through being kept in ignorance – and can arise in any of the holding worlds in which young people participate:

- home
- school
- peer group
- community
- church
- wider society, including the media and the internet.

Threats from home: parents, siblings

- For example, parents feel embarrassed around sexual topics, are silent on the issue, have a confused notion of sexuality and sexual behaviour, are over-protective of teenagers' contact with the opposite sex, put over-emphasis on 'the body beautiful', use sex themselves as a means to an end, allow non-supervised use of the internet and adult sex channels on TV, have their own unresolved sexual conflicts, feel powerless in the face of outside influences, fail to prepare young people for teenage physical development. Older siblings may also pose threats by modelling defensive sexual behaviours.

Threats from other significant adults

- For example, teachers grandparents, aunts or uncles may convey messages that are judgemental, critical and blaming of the young person. These adults may be modelling a confused sense of sexuality;

they may convey a message that it is something shameful or dangerous, or something that should be hidden. Threat also arises from adults who ignore the reality of teenage sexuality and desire for sexual self-expression.

Threats from peer groups: Friends, schoolmates

- For example, young people feel they must be doing 'what everybody else is doing'. They feel they have to live up to certain expectations if they want to avoid being excluded; for example, they must be ready to engage in activities such as 'beat the slapper' – who will have the record of how many you can kiss in one night? In order to be able to manage among their peers, for example in school, teenagers must be 'in the know' about sexual matters, they must be saying and doing the same as others. There is also the threat that arises from crude language, for example 'blow job', 'humping' or 'I'd like a piece of that'.

Threats from the Church

- Prescriptions and proscriptions from the Church about how to be and not to be make it unsafe for young people to explore their own choices and find their own authentic sexual expression. Such authoritarian messages promote mistrust in the young person about the rightness of her sexuality and lead to confusion when what her feelings and experiences tell her are at odds with Church pronouncements.
- The Catholic Church has also often conveyed that sexuality is somehow 'not right' and must be controlled – messages that lead to shame and guilt and the repression of this expression of the self.

Threats from wider society

- Information media, such as newspapers, magazines, television, radio, books, films, videos and the internet, can pose threat by, for example, bombarding young people with the need for the 'body beautiful' and detailing strict standards about what constitutes beauty.
- The porn industry, by dehumanising sexual relating, poses a major threat to mature sexual expression; a threat that research shows teenagers are increasingly being exposed to – for example, in a survey of 14–19-year-olds in five Dublin schools, 94 per cent of boys and 68

per cent of girls had viewed pornography, mostly at friends' homes (Kelly and Regan, 2001). The same research found that teenage boys view pornography as their main source of information about sex.

- Another threat arising in the holding world of wider society comes from the role of alcohol. It appears that girls behave with far less inhibition when drunk and boys read this as giving them 'permission' to have sex. At the same time, many male teenagers protectively see their own intoxication as a way of excusing their own violating sexual behaviour.

- The media tendency of using sex as a means to an end – particularly in the sale of products – poses a threat by diminishing sexuality.

- In contemporary society, the internet has major influence on young people. A serious threat that can arise from this source is the connection of sex with violence. Sadly, there are very few portrayals supporting the vision of celebratory sexual expression arising from high self-esteem and self-possession.

- A worrying development is the sexualisation of young children – particularly girls – by the advertising industry; for example, padded bras for girls too young to have breasts; thongs for eight-year olds, 'Porn Star' T-shirts for young girls, pole dancing kits for children selling in supermarkets.

Internal threats to mature sexual self-expression for teenagers

The greatest threats to young people's sexual ease and security arise from how they feel about themselves – the distance between the real and the screen self – how they experience their physicality, and what internal messages they are carrying about sexuality and sexual behaviour. In cases where there are unspoken and unresolved sexual violations, then the dawning of mature sexual expression can be an overwhelmingly terrifying prospect.

A frequent internal threat is that which arises from how young people view their bodies and their confusion of the outward physical plane with attractiveness. Sensitivity about appearance varies from those who are critical of one particular aspect but who, generally speaking, manage with the help of grooming and cosmetics to feel fairly comfortable in social situations, to those who hate their bodies and either spend endless hours in front of the mirror or avoid the mirror altogether and who dread social situations, even becoming socially phobic. The sad reality for those who are critical of their physicality is that even when they are judged as 'beautiful' or hailed as 'a film star', their own internal image of themselves blocks the reception of any genuine feedback. It is in this sense that beauty lies *not* in the eyes of the beholder but in the beheld. Individuals with doubts about their physical attractiveness either want constant reassurance of their beauty or hate when any comments – positive or negative – are made. Indeed, some individuals can become dangerously aggressive towards others or themselves when a critical remark is made.

The person who rejects her body can often develop the protective strategy of paranoia whereby when she sees someone looking at her, she automatically thinks that she is being talked about or laughed at. This projection of her own doubts about herself onto the thoughts and actions of another is a wonderful protective mechanism that, through avoidance of others, stops her experiencing rejection.

Fear of rejection in a teenager arises from earlier experiences of rejection as a child. Many people as children have suffered critical comments about their bodies or have experienced comparisons with other children seen as being more attractive. From ourselves and from clients, there are memories, for example, of being told, 'Someday you might be as good looking as your brother!', or of being labelled 'fat', 'monkey-faced', 'plain', 'short', 'lanky' and 'ugly'.

Teenagers can experience the threat of criticism not only from the adults in their holding worlds but also from their peers; in fact, adolescents can be particularly nasty towards each other in their remarks on physical appearance. Specialists in body image suggest parents can help teenagers by: accentuating the positive; by identifying and challenging their critical thinking patterns; and by helping them to learn to receive compliments. The problem with accentuating the positive is that parents are discriminating against some parts of the teenager's body in favour of others and the teenager will never be able to find a mature acceptance of himself in this way. Each teenager's body is unique in its physical make-up. Among the billions of human beings in the world there are no replicas; this fact highlights the defensiveness that underlies social images of the 'perfect' female/male body that we are all meant to emulate. Parents need to give their teenagers the understanding that not only is the body unique, it is sacred and carries every precious aspect of the teenager's being. It is only through embracing and accepting their physical difference from all others that teenagers can find security in their physical presence. Teenagers need to be given the understanding that their bodies are powerfully attractive just as they are; and that this attractiveness lies in their living presence.

It is not often recognised but compliments can pose almost as much difficulty as criticisms for a teenager who does not have a secure sense of the unconditional attract-ability of her presence. The teenager needs to be guided to understand that whether expressing a criticism or compliment, the reaction belongs to the other person and is a revelation about that other person – and the other's reaction does not reflect one iota on the young person's inherent attract-ability. Obviously, hearing a compliment is a much happier experience than hearing a criticism, but the young person needs to learn to stay separate from both and to hold on to her own deep acceptance of herself.

The responsibility lies with parents, and other significant adults in teenagers' lives, to redeem their ease with their own bodies and to practise separation of one's person from one's appearance; to resolve the confusion of attractiveness with the surface plane of one's physical appearance.

Parents would do well, too, to note the verbal messages young people give themselves about their physicality and sexuality. The parenting responsibilities of 'know your teenager' and 'be sure your teenager knows you' are particularly relevant here; with uninterrupted listening and avoidance of advice-giving or, even worse, preaching, being crucial to such knowing. Parents need to trust that young people will come up with their own solutions in the safety of unconditional love and active listening. When teenagers do ask for advice, parents need to acknowledge that they can only say what works for them and that it is for the young person to check whether what the parent is saying will help her in her unique situation. This creates equality in the communication and gives space for the teenager to find her own feet in the situation. No matter what the teenager says – for example, 'I hate my body', 'I feel so ugly', 'nobody would want me' – the parent needs to hold the young person where she is and not rush into rescue mode. Acknowledging what she is feeling and how difficult it is for her go a long way towards easing her inner suffering. Supporting her in her own solutions adds to the healing process.

Teenagers' protectors around sexuality

Just like adults, when teenagers experience themselves as being under threat, they very wisely and creatively develop protectors. Parents can get to know something of their teenagers' inner worlds by noticing the protectors they present. These protectors may cause distress, annoyance and frustration, but the parents need to understand that the protective behaviours are 'right' psychologically for the young person and that they are signalling underlying fears, self-doubts and vulnerabilities. Parents have a responsibility to guide the young person in getting beneath and uncovering what it is the protectors are alerting them to and what needs to be resolved.

Teenage protectors around sexuality, as with other dimensions of self-expression, may involve 'acting-in' or 'acting-out' behaviours. Below are listed some of the protectors that teenagers may exhibit.

Acting-in
- keeping themselves very hidden in their sexuality
- being very shy or embarrassed around sexual matters
- not communicating around sexual matters
- avoiding sexual matters
- staying in the child's place in regard to sexual matters
- 'fitting in' at all costs.

Acting-out
- being outrageous in their sexual behaviour
- being vulgar
- being 'chauvinistic'
- bragging about 'scoring'
- being smart/cynical
- being irresponsible
- being derisive
- being argumentative
- being rebellious
- being derogatory
- being aggressive

- being rejecting
- bullying others
- shaming others

The practice of safe holding of sexuality

Teenage protectors arise in response to threats coming from their inner worlds and, very significantly, in response to threats experienced in the places they live, study, pray and play. Mature responsiveness to teenagers' protectors and safe holding of sexuality are responsibilities that belong to all the adults whom teenagers encounter in their various holding worlds but, clearly, the key holding world is the family and the key influence is the parents' own relationship to their sexual self-expression.

The key dimensions of safe holding in the home involve:
- the mother's relationship to her sexual presence
- the father's relationship to his sexual presence
- the way parents interact around one another's sexual presence
- the mother's relationship to her child's sexual presence
- the father's relationship to his child's sexual presence.

How parents, and other significant adults, relate to their own sexual presence is the crucial influence on what they bring to young people around their sexual presence; all safe holding of sexuality for young people begins with safe holding for the adults themselves. Finding safe holding of their own sexual presence can be a long journey for parents; calling out as it does for commitment, awareness and persistence. But this is what safe holding of sexuality for young people actually requires. Parents cannot be credible in presenting a vision of authentic sexual self-expression to their teenagers if they themselves are operating from a screen self in their sexuality.

For both parents and teenagers there is a need for:
- acknowledgement and holding of vulnerabilities and self-doubts arising from unsafe holding
- compassionate recognition and holding of the protectors that have been developed out of necessity
- active responsiveness to what lies hidden (what aspects of sexuality that are not openly expressed)
- open addressing of identified needs.

Parents need to understand that sexuality is most powerfully held when it is responded to in the context of the *totality* of expressions available to the self. The young person is better enabled to make safe, mature sexual choices for herself when she has the physical safety to look after her body, when she has the emotional safety to follow her own feelings in a sexual situation, when she has the intellectual safety to make up her own mind about what is right for her, when she has the social safety to not conform and stay true to herself, and when she has the behavioural safety to take ownership of and responsibility for her own actions and their consequences. (See Chapter 6 for guidelines on creating safety for each of the different dimensions of self-expression.)

Safe communication around sexual matters

Many teenagers go through fears and doubts about their sexual feelings and sexual attractiveness. Young people can suffer greatly when they experience the onset of puberty later than peers, some can experience pressure to have a boy/girlfriend before they are ready for that experience, and some can go through trauma when they find themselves attracted to a member of their own gender. In the relationship between parent and teenager, the young person has all her own concerns, needs, self-doubts and protectors, but so too does the parent. Some key concerns shared by both teenagers and their parents revolve around:

- self-pleasuring
- sexual exploration/activity with another person; including issues of contraception and safe sex
- gender orientation – opposite gender or same gender.

The challenge for the parents is to be secure enough in themselves that they can create a safe atmosphere in which such issues can be raised with openness for both parties involved. Parents need to know where they stand themselves on such issues and need to have some sense of whatever defensiveness might be present for them – in other words, the parents need to be reflective about their own sexual journey and their own processes.

Such reflection can present a major challenge for parents; the survey of British parents, already referred to in Chapter 5, brought to light shyness and embarrassment on the part of both mothers and fathers on the issue of talking to teenagers about sexual matters. Mothers, generally, fared better than father: only 44 per cent of fathers broached the topic of sex with their children and 9 per cent were judged to have done a 'hopeless' job. On the other hand, 57 per cent of mothers raised the topic and 18 per cent were judged as having done an 'excellent' job, while the remaining 39 per cent were judged to have made 'a pretty good attempt'.

Some general guidelines are presented below on how parents might communicate in a safe way with their teenagers in regard to sexual matters:

- be real rather than attempting to be 'cool' or 'smart'
- be aware of, take responsibility for, and respond to your own feelings/needs/discomforts
- be direct, straightforward, honest
- be non-judgemental
- take the young person where she is and take yourself where you are
- create an atmosphere of open communication from the beginning of the child's life
- provide age-appropriate information from the beginning of the child's life
- acknowledge, value and celebrate the occurrence of physical changes – for example, the need for shaving, the development of breasts, the onset of menstruation or wet dreams
- respect the privacy of the young person and hold to appropriate boundaries
- respect the readiness of the young person for communication/ information
- treat sexuality as an integral and natural aspect of our humanness and model that naturalness
- have an attitude of celebration towards sexuality
- explore the young person's own experiences while respecting her privacy; let her tell you how she feels; give an understanding of how you feel/see things
- take whatever time is necessary
- in the case of fraught issues, such as contraception, pick an appropriate time to talk
- maximise the opportunities for communication that turn up in everyday life, such as situations/events happening to characters in soap operas.

Communication around self-pleasuring

As emphasised earlier, sexual self-expression does not necessarily involve sexual activity with another. The young person may experience her sexuality through many different means; she may, for example, experience a sense of intense physical aliveness through an activity such as swimming or dance, she may experience a strong sense of the joy of being alive through music or art or food, she may experience sexual arousal through different forms of erotica – images, art, photography, film, written materials.

The young person may also experience her sexual energy through the pleasure obtained from touching and caressing her body, particularly her genital areas. It can be very threatening for a young person to explore self-pleasuring because of, for example, adult reactions to her exploration of her body in childhood, because of the crude language often used to describe this kind of expression – such as 'wanking' or 'at yourself' – and because of the myths and fears that may still be communicated by adults, such as parents, teachers, members of the clergy, peers and media. From our discussions with groups and individuals, the following are some of the more common fears and myths that still exist around self-pleasuring:

- it's immature
- it's unhealthy
- it's just plain wrong
- it's a sin, dirty, shameful
- only boys/men masturbate
- nice girls don't touch themselves 'down there'; it's just not done for women to masturbate
- masturbation is only for kids
- it doesn't count as real sex; it's a last resort if you don't have a partner; it's demeaning if you have to
- orgasms with masturbation don't count
- you could become addicted to it
- it will harm you physically
- it reflects psychological problems.

Choice is essential in reaching authentic sexual self-expression and in order for young people to have choice, parents need to give them some facts about self-pleasuring and be open to what might be good about this kind of expression:

- it's a natural expression of sexuality
- many mature people self-pleasure
- if nothing else, it can be a healthy release from sexual tension
- feeling pleasure in this way is no different from the pleasure obtained from dancing/games, etc.
- it can enable you to learn about, and keep in touch with, your wonderful ability for sexual pleasure
- it can help you reclaim your body as *yours*; you can enjoy your body for yourself
- you can explore your body without the distraction of a partner
- it's a chance to experiment with what gives you pleasure
- it can be relaxing, fun, pure pleasure, releasing, healing.

Parents need to help the young person to make up her own mind about what is right and wrong for her, to appreciate all of her body, to honour her body for its capacity for pleasure, and to get to know and reclaim her body as being here for her pleasure.

Communication around sexual expression with another

Parents need to understand and convey to their teenagers that having the physical wherewithal to perform sexually is not the key to sexual fulfilment. Young people need to be shown that there is more involved in sexual maturity than knowing the mechanics of sexual intercourse; they need to be given some sense of the dynamics involved in eroticism, sexual desire and intimacy. It may seem paradoxical, but the key to intimacy with another is separateness; those who are self-possessed are those who have the most fulfilling sexual experiences. Self-possession, as described in earlier chapters, involves the ownership of your own needs and feelings, carrying responsibility for yourself and only yourself, being responsive towards – but not responsible for – the other person, using your own feelings as the true guide to what you do, exercising choice, taking your cues from yourself, and saying 'no' when you need to say 'no'. Such self-possession is likely to be far distant from teenagers, and parents may need to encourage them to hold off from entering into intimate sexual relations with another person until they have reached some level of inner security.

Communication around gender orientation

With the coming of adolescence, sexual attraction to another starts to become an important dimension of the lives of young people. There can be a lot of confusion for young people at this stage about where their attraction lies – with members of the opposite or the same gender – and sadly there is not often the safe holding that would enable them to make a free and authentic choice for themselves. The crucial factor is *choice*; the focus of the parent needs to be on enabling the young person to figure out what is right for her. As with all other forms of self-expression, reaching for free choice involves the young person coming into conscious awareness of the threats that may be present and the consequent protective strategies she may have had to create.

One of the major threats against free choice is that, in the holding world of society, individuals who make the choice of same-gender attraction are considered as 'them' who are different from 'us' who make the choice for the opposite gender; with 'them' being seen as, for example:

- making a spectacle of themselves with their parades and their form of dress
- as all being paedophiles; as being transvestites
- as being dangerous to others
- as being criminal
- as all being promiscuous
- as being anti-Church
- as being wrong and sinful in their way
- as all coming from unhappy families
- as being abnormal/deviant/sick
- as not being able 'to help it' because it's biological.

As a result of such defensive reactions, attraction to members of the same gender can breed huge fear: for example, fear of being rejected, isolated, labelled, hounded, mocked, shamed, excluded, discriminated against, and cast out by family and friends.

Because the parents themselves may share these threats and fears, they may find it very difficult to provide the safe holding that the young person making a same-gender choice needs. The key elements of safe holding include:

- avoiding all judgement
- listening actively without interruption
- avoiding efforts to try to 'fix it'
- letting the young person come to her own answers
- making sure that love is not withdrawn through, for example, silence, sulking, aggression, attempts to control, punishing, displays of disappointment
- showing compassion for the conflict the young person is very likely experiencing
- avoiding analysis of the reasons 'why'.

It is crucially important in the relationship between the parent and the young person that the actual person of the son or daughter is not confused with the choice that is being made. The young person needs to know that: 'I make a choice but I'm not my choice; my choice is one dimension of my expression of my self.' The young person needs to know from the adults that their primary concern always is: 'What is the quality of your lived experience?' The young person needs to know, without question, that it is her presence that matters and that her presence is separate from any behaviour that she may exhibit. The young person needs to hear 'may you find the *person* of your dreams' rather than 'may you find the *man/woman* of your dreams'.

In her own relationship with herself, the young person needs to be supported and encouraged to:
- recognise the uniqueness of her own story
- make decisions based on her own feelings rather than conforming to the needs/expectations of others
- understand that the only approval that finally matters is her own approval of herself
- realise that her life was given to her for her good, for her own wellbeing and fulfilment
- realise that the only responsibility that can be carried is that towards her own self
- show loving responsiveness to what life is throwing up for her
- honour herself in all of the self's expressions.

CHAPTER NINE

Teenagers in the holding world of education

- The 'inner course' determines the outer course
- Creating a safe learning environment
- A sense of belonging and its influence on school achievement
- Teenagers are not their examination results
- Homework is for adults as much as for teenagers
- Bullying: A blight on teenagers' lives
  - *Taking action for yourself: The mature response to bullying*
  - *Creating a safe environment for action for yourself*
- Lost in transition!

The 'inner course' determines the outer course

Many parents hold the strong belief that it is teenagers' progress in school that will determine their progress as adults. But experience shows that there are many highly educated adults who exhibit a low level of emotional and social maturity. External conditions, such as education, status, wealth, gender, age and position of responsibility, are not indicators of maturity; the crucial factor is the state of a person's inner world – the level of conscious awareness a person has about the threats they are experiencing and the protective strategies they are creating in the face of these threats. Tending to your inner world – the 'inner course' – has not been a priority for adults in our society, and this has resulted in the kinds of immature behaviour – such as snobbery, greed, avarice, bullying, passivity and depersonalisation of individuals – that have become so evident in recent times. Progress comes from maturity, where the emphasis is on relationship depth – on the support of individuality, equality, fairness, justice, inclusiveness, and on the provision of opportunities for each person to maximise their potential.

On the journey to maturity, parents need to put the focus on the inner course of teenagers rather than on the outer scholastic course. When teenagers are secure and confident within, their outer progress is also assured, but when they doubt themselves – feel inferior, feel controlled by parents, feel unable to reveal their own needs and aspirations – then, inevitably, their outer progress will be hampered. Furthermore, parents need to be wary that the son or daughter who conforms to the educational and career wishes of others and who achieves highly according to others' expectations is not likely to feel fulfilled. Indeed, those young people who conform rather than follow their own path are often masking an inner conflict that they dare not reveal for fear of disappointing or upsetting their parents or of evoking aggressive responses.

Creating a safe learning environment

The school and further and higher educational institutions constitute an important holding world for young people. In order to create safe holding for the teenager to proceed with the inner course of internal ease and security, alongside the outer scholastic course, the adults in the educational world need to relate in the following way with the young people with whom they are involved:

- the young person's presence needs to be seen as completely separate from his scholastic attainments
- teenagers need to feel that they belong in their classrooms and in their schools/institutions; they need to feel that they have their own recognised place
- the relationship between the teacher/lecturer and the young person needs always to take priority over any scholastic issues
- parents and teachers/lecturers need to watch out for young people and be alert to indications of inner insecurity – for example, timidity, bullying, passivity, aggression, apathy and perfectionism
- parents and teachers/lecturers need to ensure that learning continues to be the adventure it was when the young people were infants
- the knowledge that the young person may acquire must not be confused with the young person's innate intelligence

- all young people need to be recognised as always being deeply intelligent in how they deal with the worlds in which they find themselves
- parents and teachers/lecturers need to convey without ambiguity that success and failure are two sides of the one coin of learning
- parents and teachers/lecturers need to convey without ambiguity that it is effort rather than outcome that matters
- teenagers need guidance and support when it comes to making choices around further and higher education and future occupation/career.

A sense of belonging and its influence on school achievement

Parents and teachers/lecturers can become concerned when, from their perspective, young people academically *underachieve*. How underachievement is defined is an important consideration because what is underachievement in one person's eyes can be achievement, or, indeed, overachievement in another's eyes. Underachievement is most usefully defined from the perspective of the teenager himself – as his sense of not realising his potential – rather than from outside expectations.

It is in the understanding of the true nature of underachievement that progress towards achievement is likely to develop. When underachievement is perceived as being caused by the teenager being 'weak' or 'slow' or 'lazy', the possibilities for progress are greatly reduced as no belief is now being shown in the teenager's vast intelligence, wisdom and limitless capacity to learn. Belief in their ever-present intelligence is central to motivating young people to realise their potential. The labelling of teenagers serves no purpose for them; however, it may serve some protective purpose for the adults who do the labelling by letting them off the hook of responsibility. The truth is that scholastic underachievement on the part of teenagers is very likely pointing to a more serious underachievement on the part of the parents and/or on the part of the educators. Teenagers' prime need – like that of adults – is to be loved and to love, and they need to feel they belong to their homes, to their schools and to their peer group. It is when these belonging needs are not met, that they can manifest in school underachievement. Almost always it is some form of lack of belonging that underlies persistent underachievement among teenagers and it is in addressing that emotional deprivation that teenagers can become psycho-socially ready for achievement. It is the responsibility of parents and teachers to provide the safe holding for these belonging needs but, sadly, instead of safe holding, teenagers can often experience either over-belonging or under-belonging. It is easy to see how underachievement could be an apt substitute response to over-belonging where the parent does everything for the teenager. Likewise, it makes sense that a teenager under pressure to achieve by parents might rebel through underachievement. It is also very understandable that teenagers who experience lack of any belonging through persistent emotional and physical neglect might have other things on their mind besides academic learning.

Curiously, parents and educators rarely worry about teenagers who *overachieve* but the fact is that overachievement is as serious as underachievement in the wellbeing of young people. Overachievement can often represent an attempt by a teenager to attract, in a substitute way, a parent whose own self-image is tied up with academic performance. It can also happen that the teenager is reacting to parents who feel aggrieved at their own lack of educational opportunities and are over-determined that their children should achieve. Overachievement can be linked to the kind of under-belonging whereby parents live their lives through their teenagers' achievements, and woe betide the young person should he ever disappoint. Sometimes, overachievement stems from no-belonging with the teenager attempting desperately to rise above his neglectful circumstances; this reaction can develop into an addiction to success, leading to him neglecting himself and, later on in adulthood, to neglect of a marital partner and children.

In order for young people to achieve their potential across the full spectrum of their capabilities – physical, emotional, social, intellectual, behavioural, sexual, creative and spiritual – they need to have the security of unconditional belonging in the holding worlds that are critical for them – home, school, educational institution and community. It is the provision of this safe holding that provides the inner solidity for young people to achieve outwardly in the educational world and beyond.

Teenagers are not their examination results

In late summer, Irish media are full of the results of the Leaving Certificate with headlines such as: 'All As – the brainiest student in Ireland.' It needs to be recognised that such reporting constitutes a major threat to young people in the holding world of society. The threat comes from the confusion of intelligence with examination results and the acceptance of performance as the measure of a person's worth. All adults in the holding worlds of young people need to understand that an examination result is no measure of that person's worth or capability; a person's worth and capability are a given and do not need to be proved. Marks on an examination paper or feedback on scholastic work need to be seen for what they are – communications to students about the level of knowledge and skills they have shown. Such communications are, of course, important and when feedback is accurate, realistic and honest, it enables the student by charting his progress in the specific knowledge area examined. The provision of realistic, honest and accurate feedback on what they have attained is a mark of respect and care. Parents and educators may sometimes dilute the reality of lack of progress in the knowledge-area examined for fear of causing a blow to the student's self-esteem. But it is the lack of honesty that causes the blow as it shows no acknowledgement of the student's capacity to come to grips with and resolve difficulties that may be arising in his scholastic life.

Accurate feedback does not confuse scholastic outcome with the person of the student. When confusion of the outcome and the person occurs – as in the examples below – major unsafety is created for the young person around open, real expression of his intelligence:

- 'You failed that test.'
- 'You're a disappointment to us.'
- 'You were highly successful.'
- 'You're a poor student.'
- 'You're weak in mathematics.'
- 'You're a credit to the school.'
- 'You're the brainiest person in Ireland.'

In order to create the kind of safe holding that enables teenagers to give full expression of their intelligence, it is essential that the message goes out, loud and clear, that no student can be equated with an examination result, no matter what that result is – poor, average, fail, pass, honours or outstanding. Every young person needs to be able to shout from the rooftops: 'I'm not an examination result!' An examination result is *not* a measure of the young person's worth, intelligence, creativity or individuality – but, sadly, few students view examinations in this way and instead experience them as threats to their sense of self. The truth is that it is not examination success that determines progress but maturity. Research shows that, in our current society, the highest academic performers are those students who gain entrance to medicine, and yet medical doctors have the highest suicide rate, the highest level of alcohol and drug addiction, and the highest incidence of marital and family breakdown – indicating not progress but inner turmoil.

Another critical issue in maintaining safe holding while giving feedback on progress is not to confuse knowledge with intelligence. Knowledge levels are a reflection of a variety of conditions – such as learning opportunity, motivation, interest, attitude, support and modelling – but are no reflection of intelligence. Sadly, many young people see themselves through received labels, such as 'failure', 'average', 'weak', 'clever' or 'gifted', and, as a result, their sense of self is greatly under threat. What is not often appreciated is that the young person who believes he is the 'clever one' is just as emotionally at risk as the one who believes he is 'useless' – the former teenager is continually under strain to live up to his pedestal position, and his defensive strategy of high performance and perfectionism is just as strong a defence as the avoidance of academic challenge shown by the latter student.

It is incumbent on parents and educators to create the kind of safe educational environment in which examinations are regarded as an adventure rather than a source of threat to one's sense of self.

Homework is for adults as much as for teenagers

In our work, we have heard children as young as six years of age complain about being 'all stressed out by tests'. It is not the tests in themselves that threaten children's wellbeing, but how the significant adults in their lives respond to the outcomes of those tests. The two key responses in ensuring wellbeing among young people are unconditional love of them for their person and belief in their capability to understand and take charge of the world in which they live. Communicating belief means communicating to all teenagers in homes and in educational institutions how wonderfully intelligent each one of them is and letting them know that level of knowledge of a subject, or results in a test or examination, neither add to nor detract from their intelligence.

It is noteworthy that toddlers typically love to test themselves, and the experiences of failure and success do not deter them from their risk-taking, natural curiosity and love of learning, yet by early childhood many have lost these qualities. Such a tragic change happens when the toddler encounters adults who because of their own early distressing experiences of learning buried these qualities in themselves in an effort to avoid recurrences of hurt. Of course, parents and educators want young people to progress in their academic and career lives, but this is much more likely to happen when the adults themselves are risk-takers, do not confuse their person with examination results, success or status, and do not threaten doom and gloom on those teenagers who are not academically thriving.

When the learning environment threatens the wellbeing of the young person, the more typical strategies for offsetting hurt and rejection are:

- avoidance of scholastic effort
- aggression in response to pressure from parents/educators
- perfectionism
- going for the average.

When teenagers manifest such protective responses, it is important that the significant adults in their lives do their 'homework' of reflecting on the attitudes to learning that prevail in the home, in the educational setting and among the young person's peers.

It is not often recognised, but it is very important to understand, that perfectionism, the striving always to be top of the class, is as much a protective strategy as avoidance of effort and is equally calling out for parental 'homework'. The essential response to lack of motivation and lack of effort around school learning and examination preparation is to talk *with* the teenager. Any hint of labelling as 'lazy' or 'irresponsible', or any displays of impatience, irritability or over-anxiety on the part of parents or educators will lead to the young person pulling down the shutters and not revealing what lies behind his challenging behaviours.

Naturally, it is worrying and often puzzling for parents when their teenager is avoiding scholastic work or showing aggression around any attempts to raise the subject. However, while the situation is worrying for parents, it is important to realise that it is likely to be even more worrying for the young person. Young people want to get the most out of life, but academic and career progress are a poor second best to being loved for self and being encouraged and supported to discover their own unique way of being and their own path in the world. When the naturally occurring love of learning is no longer present, this is a sure indication that something is amiss in the relationship between the young person and some significant adult and, unless that rift in relationship is resolved, the young person may not recover the love of learning that has been repressed. Wisely, the young person tries to offset threats and it is only when safety has been restored that the teenager will be likely to begin to take the risk again to learn and explore.

It is crucial that parents and teachers do not jeopardise their relationships with teenagers because of scholastic work and examinations. When it is relationships that are paramount in homes and in the educational holding world, young people tend to maintain their natural curiosity, risk-taking, testing of themselves and love of learning. It is important for adults to realise that a principal motivation for young people – as it is for all of us – is to express their individuality; putting pressure on the young person to be the same as other students is always counterproductive.

Parents do need to ensure that their teenagers fulfil the responsibilities of being a student – and part of those responsibilities is the effective completion of school homework. But the way a parent approaches the issue of responsibility needs serious consideration, because, ironically, it may be that it is because the parents themselves are not fulfilling their responsibilities of 'homework' that the young person is resistant to his homework. Take the case of the mother who was very distressed by the behaviour of her 14-year old son when it came to getting him to do his homework. Over several years, he had thrown temper tantrums and shown great defiance to her attempts to make him do his homework; his defiance recently escalating to physically lashing out. The teenager revealed that he hated school, hated homework and could not wait to leave school. It emerged that when he was four years of age he had engaged in an exploration of the contents of his father's office, only to be physically beaten and harshly corrected for 'making a mess'. The mature parent knows that 'making a mess' is central to children's quest to make sense of and to understand the complex worlds in which they live. If the father had done his homework and with patience and understanding enquired into the child's explorations, he would have won the child's heart and reinforced his natural curiosity and eagerness to learn. Because such parental homework was not done what followed was a repression of those core qualities in the child with the resultant hate of learning and homework. Of course, parents need to maintain definite boundaries around their own physical and emotional wellbeing (see Chapter 7) but, alongside boundaries, parents need to try to uncover the hidden emotional turmoil underlying the challenging behaviours being exhibited by the young person.

It must be recognised that a teenager's difficulties with homework can have sources other than in the home. We have heard from many students stories of humiliation and ridicule in classrooms in their teenage years. If it is the responsibility of parents to do their 'homework' of creating quality relationships in the home, teachers/lecturers also have the 'homework' of creating a safe environment for learning within their respective educational settings. The more that the significant adults in teenagers' lives take on their responsibilities, the more the teenagers will follow suit. When a safe learning environment is not present, then the reasons for the educators' failure to do their 'homework' needs to be addressed urgently.

When young people show lack of commitment to their studies, parents and educators in their frustration can often respond with labels such as 'waster', 'lazy', 'hyperactive', 'ungrateful', 'bored', 'irresponsible', 'difficult', 'aggressive' or 'distracted'. While the common perception of young people is that they are 'troublesome', the truth is that they are crying out for help and, sadly, that cry so often goes unheard. When it is unsafe to speak the truth of what is happening in their relationships with parents and educators, young people unconsciously, and creatively, find substitute ways of expressing their inner turmoil. The hope is that some adult out there will spot the deeper meaning of their 'difficult' attitude to their studies and will offer the love, support and belief in them that will enable them to resolve their distress.

There is nearly always a double meaning to words and actions – the literal meaning and the deeper metaphorical meaning. The crucial homework here for parents is to seek the deeper meaning. When teachers and parents react only to the literal meaning of teenagers' troubling behaviours, the likelihood is that the teenagers will be blamed, castigated and considered deserving of a 'good telling off' – all responses that serve only to exacerbate the young person's inner turmoil and to escalate the difficult behaviours. When the deeper metaphorical intention of the troubling behaviours is sought, an entirely different response emerges. The deeper meaning will be unique to each young person, and it is only by talking *with* him that the hidden intention of the behaviours will begin to emerge.

Below are listed some possible metaphorical meanings for some of the typical complaints about young people voiced by parents and educators, but only the young people concerned can verify the accuracy of the interpretations.

TABLE 9.1: POSSIBLE METAPHORICAL MEANINGS FOR SOME TYPICAL COMPLAINTS

Typical complaint of parent/educator	Possible metaphorical meaning for teenager (what lies hidden that is seeking to emerge)
'waster'	I see myself as a waste of time and quality emotional time was wasted in family.
'no homework'	Parents did not do their homework – they did not create a secure and loving place; I don't feel at home with myself.
'lazy'	No energy given to relationships in the family; no energy for myself.
'difficult'	Things are 'difficult' at home and within myself.
'hyperactive'	Too much going on at home; no sense of peace within myself.
'distracted'	Family life is completely 'off track'; I'm not attracted to myself.
'bored'	What has been 'bored' into me about who I am has hurt me deeply. I have no interest in myself.
'tired'	Parents/teachers are 'tired' of me; I'm tired of myself.
'irresponsible'	Parents/teachers do not exhibit responsible behaviours. I struggle with taking responsibility for myself.

continued on next page ⟶

Typical complaint of parent/educator	Possible metaphorical meaning for teenager (what lies hidden that is seeking to emerge)
'absent'	Parents/teachers are not present to me; I am not present to myself.
'aggressive'	Parents/teachers are hostile to me; I hate myself.
'in another world'	The real world is too painful a place to be; I have no sense of inner worth (world).
'failing'	There have been many relationship failures in my home and school; I see myself as a failure.
'ungrateful'	I have never felt appreciated at home or in school; I have no appreciation of myself.

Considerable sensitivity and patience are needed when helping young people to reveal and resolve their inner troubled worlds. Educators and parents need to co-operate in offering the young person unconditional regard, understanding, compassion and support. Where older teenagers are involved, they can be championed to stand up for themselves and live their own lives and not the lives of their parents or teachers.

Bullying: A blight on teenagers' lives

It is a sad reality that one of the major threats that can arise for young people in the educational holding world is bullying behaviour from peers and/or educators. Bullying can be a blight on teenagers' lives – on their sense of self, on their confidence, on their physical, sexual, emotional and social development, and on their overall wellbeing; it can also affect their educational and career progress dramatically and, in extreme cases, can lead to suicidal feelings or to suicide.

The term 'bullying' covers a range of threatening responses that undermine, upset, insult, isolate, intimidate, exclude, terrify, physically hurt, sexually violate or emotionally torment those who are bullied. Increasingly sophisticated communication technology has sadly allowed the possibilities for bullying behaviour to extend beyond the immediate environment of class/lecture room or neighbourhood.

Despite anti-bullying initiatives, school policies, parental awareness and educational interventions, each new cohort of teenagers experiences similar humiliating and intimidating experiences as the previous cohort.

It is particularly worrying that the majority of parents and educators appear to remain unaware of the extent of this assault on teenagers' wellbeing. A question that is arises here is: 'How is it that teenagers do not feel that their parents and teachers will care and take due action around their frightening experiences of being bullied?' One possible answer is that parents and educators often ascribe the bullying to some quality in the teenager being bullied – physical appearance, school performance, or physical, social or intellectual disability. If parents and educators imply blame or overtly blame the person being bullied then, of course, teenagers will hide their shame at being bullied. No teenager invites bullying; such a perception is abandonment and, because it does not get to the source of the bullying, it will never bring resolution.

The reality is that the bullying behaviour is 100 per cent about the individuals who bully. It needs to be communicated unambiguously that the teenagers who are bullied are not the problem – the problem is with the individuals who are doing the bullying. Once the source of the problem is placed where it belongs then some 'homework' can be done about what is happening in the bully's inner world and what help he needs to resolve his inner conflict so that he no longer poses a threat to other people. It must be remembered that it is not always another young person who perpetrates the bullying behaviour, teachers, lecturers and other adults can also bully.

Parents and teachers need to be alert to the signs that a teenager is being bullied. The more typical indications are that the teenager suddenly becomes touchy, moody, irritable and angry; their academic achievement may deteriorate unexpectedly; they may be carefree during holiday time but exhibit misery during school-time; they may refuse to talk about friends or school; they may look for extra pocket money in order to placate the bullies; they may want to be driven to and from school for protection; they may develop physical symptoms of illness so that they do not to have to go to school. Parents and educators need to be wary of assuming that the above signs always indicate the presence of bullying; there may be other sources located in the home (for example, marital discord) or within the educational setting (for example, the teenager feels he is being picked on by a teacher). Only the teenager himself can verify what is going on in his life underneath the flag of distress being flown.

Taking action for yourself: The mature response to bullying

A truth that parents and educators need to communicate to young people is that *teenagers who bully are fearful* and are urgently crying out for help. It is both a comforting and empowering experience for young people to learn that those peers who bully them are masking their fears and insecurities, and are far from being as powerful as they try to portray. Efforts to help and encourage young people to 'stand up for themselves' will be much more likely to succeed when the young people are given an understanding that the source of the bullying lies with the person who bullies and the source is always about the bully's own fears, vulnerabilities and self-doubt. With this understanding, the young person can be enabled to respond maturely to the experience of being bullied; the essence of mature responding being to 'take action for yourself'. When action for yourself is the focus, the young person now does not have to deal with or struggle with the bully – an impossible task – but can focus on what *is* in his power – to take care of himself.

There are no set answers to what the 'action for yourself' should be; the answer needs to emerge from consideration of the young person's feelings, experiences and considerations so he can make a real choice about what is best for his wellbeing. Making choices for his wellbeing is a power that no bully can take from him. Some possibilities regarding action for yourself are that the teenager show *absolutely* no response; that he report the bullying to an adult who will listen and act maturely and persistently to restore safety to his world; that he assertively say, 'No, I'm not responding to that taunt' (but only when physically safe to do so). Action for yourself takes the young person out of the bully's space and keeps him in his own space where nobody has power over him. When the young person finds himself taking action against the bully, the situation only escalates and the bully is likely to be a lot more practised in the bullying world.

Creating a safe environment for action for yourself

The creation of a safe holding world in the educational environment requires a double-sided action: the institution of an anti-bullying campaign balanced with an anti-passivity campaign. Bullying thrives only in situations where it is either actively supported or indirectly supported through passivity. Active support is where other teenagers participate by 'cheering on' bullying behaviour. Passive support is where those teenagers who witness a peer being bullied do nothing about it, possibly out of fear of being bullied themselves. Young people who bully do not attempt to do so with peers who can take action for themselves and who will not stand idly by when they witness another being bullied. The saying that 'where good men do nothing in the face of evil, evil thrives' applies equally to teenagers who do nothing in the face of bullying behaviour.

Bullying is clearly a serious threat to the wellbeing of the young person targeted, but an equally serious threat arises when the individual who has been bullied does not feel safe enough to report the demeaning of his presence that is taking place. Teenagers who witness a significant adult in their lives – for example, parent, teacher, sports coach – employing bullying as a means of relating will not dare report being bullied by a peer or by another adult to that person. Equally, a teenager who witnesses a parent or teacher being passive in the face of intimidation will know that it is not safe to report bullying to that person.

The first action in the creation of a safe environment is for adults to understand that if they are unable to champion themselves then they will not be able to take mature action if and when they hear about a teenager being bullied. Until parents and teachers resolve their own issues of bullying or passivity, teenagers who are bullied will wisely keep their trauma to themselves. The sad reality is that, too often, their diaries know more about the tough realities of their lives than do their parents, siblings, teachers or friends.

The responsibility lies with parents and educators to recognise, understand, monitor, challenge, confront and maturely resolve bullying and passivity no matter where they find it; when such an attitude is not present, then the parents and educators need more help than those teenagers they are not safeguarding.

One strategy that a school, for example, could introduce to counter passivity is to have a strategically placed bullying-report box through which both witnesses and targets could anonymously provide information on bullying incidents. It is incumbent on all school staff to create a culture where there is persistent active support for the reporting of bullying and where a strong, clear message is sent out that the school will not tolerate any member – student or staff – being bullied. Teachers need to ensure that they themselves do not engage in bullying behaviours either towards students or towards colleagues; not only because this creates huge threat in the environment but also because double standards support teenagers bullying other teenagers. The provision of a course on assertiveness could help young people to understand what is involved in staying separate from the other's behaviours, in keeping the focus on their own wellbeing needs and in taking action that matches those needs. Parent Associations need to be very active in promoting the actions that create a safe school environment for young people. The involvement of the parents of the teenagers doing the bullying and of those teenagers who stand idly by is critical to any intervention because frequently the sources of a teenager's bullying behaviour lie within the holding world of home.

An effective anti-bullying campaign involves having an understanding of the bullying behaviour as a strong protective strategy on the part of the bully. As well as safeguarding the victims of the bullying there needs to be also a commitment to providing the young person doing the bullying with the necessary help that will enable him to uncover what it is he is protecting against and to find more open, mature ways of resolving whatever inner conflicts he is experiencing.

Lost in transition!

Those teenagers who continue on from school into the wider world of further and higher education face many new challenges, both educationally and emotionally, but often arrive in that world with a confused sense of self. It is to their credit that in spite of possible ongoing emotional turmoil the great majority of young people manage the transition to third-level schooling effectively. A recent report (2010) by the Higher Education Authority shows that the proportion of new entrants in 2007–2008 who were not present one year later was 15 per cent on average across all sectors and National Framework of Qualification (NFQ) levels. But it is important to uncover what is happening for the 15 per cent of first-year students who drop out of third-level education. Indeed, that deeper *examination* of their sense of self, of their parents' relationship with them and of their relationship with their peers is far more important than the end-of-year academic examination. It must also be recognised that teenagers who continue on into the wider educational world are not only facing an educational transition but very often are also facing the major challenge of leaving home; a challenge also faced by young people entering the wider world of work. Leaving home is a prospect that some young people look forward to, while others view it with fear and trepidation.

The preparation of young people to manage their own welfare is a key parenting responsibility. Sons and daughters who have had the good fortune to have been given the opportunities to stand on their own two capable feet from their childhood years can really enjoy the adventure of leaving the nest and taking responsibility for themselves. However, because many adults themselves find it a highly uncomfortable challenge to lean on themselves, teenagers very often do not get the encouragement and support they need to become independent and can become lost in the transition from home to wider holding worlds of further education and work.

Separateness, the ability to stand one your own two feet, and the letting go of dependence on parents, form the basis for maturity; challenges that can be as daunting for parents as for young people. Young people are not immune to the emotional difficulties of their parents and, when parents do not work on the development of separateness from their children, it is not then emotionally safe for young people to assert their need to fly the nest; on the contrary, what is likely to happen is that the young people conform to their parents' dependence on them and show no eagerness or willingness to separate out from family. Those young people whose parents have done everything for them will encounter a sense of helplessness when away from home and are likely to be considerably unsettled – perhaps returning home every weekend or finding the transition too frightening and dropping out of college altogether and returning home. Young people who have been dominated and deprived of opportunities to develop their own initiative, to make their own decisions, and to do things their own individual way, are likely to continue to live out their parents' projections or, when out of sight of their parents, they may rebel by doing little or no study or over-indulging in the social side of college life. Whether they conform or rebel, these young people are struggling to find their inner solidity and it may take a series of crises to bring into the open what a challenge it is for them to live their own lives and cut the umbilical cord to their family of origin.

Parents can sometimes worry that sons and daughters living away from home are 'partying all of the time'. This is not as common as some parents believe – and indeed some partying is essential as part of emotional and social development – but when it does occur it needs to be understood as a substitute behaviour covering up issues such as being unhappy in choice of course but being fearful of disappointing or upsetting parents or causing outrage by making a change.

Those young people who continue to live at home also face the challenge of independence and separateness. There can be a danger that the child-parent relationship is maintained and the graduation to an adult-adult relationship is not encouraged or supported. Of course, it is not essential to leave home in order to find independence; the crucial influence on whether or not young people learn to stand on their own two feet is the nature of the relationship with their parents. It certainly is the case that out of their inner distress some parents foster dependence rather than independence, and staying at home under such circumstances impedes the mature development of the young person. When this is the case, both parents and teenager have to face the challenge of reviewing the nature of the relationship between them; a challenge with which they may well need outside assistance and support.

For all teenagers – whether living at home or away – the important issue is that there has been a parent-child history characterised by freedom, trust, discipline, mutual respect, separateness and independence. Teenagers cannot move overnight from being dependent children to being independent young adults. The fostering of freedom and responsibility from their earliest days is what prepares young people to handle maturely the transitions with which they are faced. (The final chapter of the book considers in more detail the parents' responsibility to let go of their young adult offspring and the young people's responsibility to take leave of their parents.) But if there has not been such a history, all is not lost; the opportunities for change are always present and, with support and guidance, parents and teenagers can rise to the challenges involved.

While the majority of young people who go on to college manage the educational challenges involved, a significant number experience difficulties. There are many reasons why some young people do well in college, others struggle through it and yet others leave the field altogether. It is important for both parents and the young people themselves to bear in mind that there are many paths to a challenging and satisfying life and that a third-level degree is not the holy grail that it is often made out to be. There are numerous examples of individuals who did not achieve academically but who have contributed enormously to the advancement of society; perhaps the most famous example being Einstein who failed his German polytechnic entrance examination twice and only scraped through at his third and final attempt.

Among those who struggle, the nub of the problem is likely to be the extent to which they have a strong sense of self (see Chapter 2). Young people may cross the threshold of college with a strong sense of self, a crystallised sense of self or a confused sense of self. The finding of answers to questions – such as 'Who am I?'; 'What is life all about?'; 'What is my path in life?'; 'How do I become socially confident?'; 'How do I manage the myriad of feelings and drives that are happening within me?' – is more critical to a satisfying and challenging life than application to third-level studies.

Those young people who have had the benefit of a mature family holding world will already have been asking these questions and will have found some answers leading to a growing strong sense of self; college for them is a challenge and an adventure and they do not encounter any great difficulties. Those young people with a crystallised sense of self tend to be serious students, keen to fulfil the expectations of their parents; they, too, tend to do well in college but are less able to take up and enjoy the social opportunities and challenges of college life. At some point in their lives, these young people will need to face the question 'Whose life am I living?', sadly their emancipation may not come until much later in life. But it is those young people who come to college with a confused sense of self who struggle most during college years and who are most likely to drop out. Considerable understanding and patience is needed on the part of parents, educators and other significant adults for these unsettled young people; responses such as aggression, judgement, criticism, condemnation, despair and comparisons with others serve only to aggravate their inner turmoil. Certainly, parents need to set clear boundaries around their financing of the young person's education and be prepared to withdraw funds if the young person shows no willingness to try to resolve the issues blocking him from application to studies. These young people need guidance and support to reflect on the necessary identity questions. This 'inner course' of knowing the self may need a year or two of soul-searching before the young person is ready to apply himself to third-level studies and career development. For the more bewildered young person, identity confusion may go on for several years and may only get resolved through professional guidance.

CHAPTER TEN

Teenagers who are troubled and troublesome

- Behaviours that cause alarm
- The nature of the inner turmoil of teenagers
- Troublesome behaviour comes from inner turmoil
  - *Some shadow behaviours of adults*
  - *Some shadow behaviours of teenagers*
- Responding to teenage turmoil
- Turmoil arising from experiences of rejection

Behaviours that cause alarm

A survey carried out by the National Suicide Research Foundation in 2004 of almost 4,000 students aged 15–17 revealed 'a hidden population of Irish teenagers with significant mental health problems who are slipping through the healthcare net' (Sullivan et al., 2004). Twenty-seven per cent of the young people surveyed reported serious personal, emotional, behavioural or mental health problems. Less than one-fifth had tried to get professional help. Sometimes the inner turmoil of young people is hidden in 'lives of quiet desperation'. There are also those young people whose inner turmoil is expressed in more overt behaviours that cause trouble for others and who, as a result, are more likely to come to the attention of professionals. The troubled and troublesome behaviours exhibited by teenagers can sometimes be so severe as to cause serious alarm. The kinds of troubled behaviour that parents most often worry about are:

- addictive responses
- attention-deficit and hyperactivity
- 'out of control' behaviour

- self-harming
- suicide threats and attempts
- depression
- 'schizophrenic-type' behaviour
- anti-social behaviour
- extreme shyness
- constant lying.

The nature of the inner turmoil of teenagers

This chapter and the three following it – concerned with specific troubled and troublesome behaviours that cause most alarm to parents – are based on a psycholsocial model of the sources of human distress. In the psychosocial model, the sources of human distress can be traced to the human condition – we are all born to human parents and encounter other adults in our early holding worlds who, because of their own inner unresolved distress, are not in a position to offer us the unconditional love and recognition that we long for and deserve. The good news is that while relationships are the source of our difficulties, relationships are also the source of our healing. Ultimately, it is my own unconditional loving of myself that leads to the resolution of inner distress but loving relating from others is crucial to that process.

It is not easy for parents and other adults to look to their own ways of relating – both to themselves and to children – and it is understandable that in a defensive effort to avoid that challenge, the focus can be diverted onto the young people, often leading them to being labelled as suffering from some 'disorder' or 'syndrome'. When a young person's inner turmoil is seen as a syndrome or disorder, the suggestion is that there is something 'wrong' with her, and no effort is then made to enquire into the nature of the net of relationships in the different holding worlds in which she lives – home, school and community. But without such an enquiry – in the context of a 'therapeutic alliance', whether this be with parents or a professional – there can be no insight into the possible causes, intentions or meaning of the young person's emotional experiences.

In our clinical experience, all human behaviour, no matter what its nature, makes sense and has a psychological 'rightness' to it; human behaviour deserves a definition that acknowledges its always wise and creative purpose. This is not to deny that one person's troubled behaviour can pose a threat to the wellbeing of others, but that the threat is never intentional. For example, a mother's depressive behaviours can be a threat to the wellbeing of her children because she is not in a fit emotional state to nurture them in the ways they need. Likewise, a father's aggression poses threat to the safety of other family members, and action needs to be taken to ensure their safety. Anyone attempting to help the person in turmoil – whether parent or child – needs to hold simultaneously the psychological 'rightness' of the behaviour for the person herself and the social threat posed for others by the presenting distressing behaviour. When only the social threat of the person's protective actions is seen, the danger is that that person will be labelled as having a disorder or judged as 'mad', 'bad' or 'sad'. When the sense that lies behind all behaviour is recognised, it is more likely that the disturbing behaviours will be responded to compassionately, and that there will be an accompanying determination to ensure that any threat to another's safety is minimised or eliminated.

The inner turmoil of those 15–17 year olds whose distress had gone undetected (described at the start of the chapter) was manifesting itself in such defensive responses as depression, anxiety, self-harming and alcohol excess. The term 'disorder' misses the intelligence of such behaviours. In defining these patterns of behaviour, it is important that the definition reflects their meaning; such a definition will point the way towards the kind of intervention required.

It can be very difficult for parents and other concerned adults to hear what the young person may be trying to express through their outward distressing behaviour. In order to be able to listen, it is crucial that the parents do not take on the blame; the important issue is not to pinpoint where the parents 'went wrong', but rather to indentify how the teenager can be helped to 'put right' whatever the underlying turmoil may be. The outer behaviours are the teenager's wise creation and when read as such can lead to the most effective responsiveness.

For example, the teenager exhibiting depression may be signalling dimensions of the self – intelligence, zest for life, curiosity, sexuality – that have been suppressed because they dare not be shown within the holding worlds of home, school or community. Anxiety may signal the fear of expressing aspects of the self that parents or teachers or other significant adults may have severely punished – for example, the right to fail or the right to have your own opinion. Self-harming may signal a sense of having been 'harmed' through being blocked by the defensive responses of some significant adult in the young person's life. Over-indulgence in alcohol can often be a means of boosting confidence by a young person who possesses little real belief in him or her self. Whatever the symptoms, their origins lie in the nature of the relationships experienced with parents or teachers or other significant adults or with peers. Turmoil in a young person is an invitation for all members of the family – and in some cases, members of the school – to reflect on their own ways of relating to others. It is crucial that the flags of distress are responded to with understanding and compassion, and with a determination to enable the young person to resolve her inner turmoil; if these efforts are not present, then the troubling and troublesome behaviours escalate in frequency and intensity.

When teenagers are in inner turmoil, their outer behaviours can be very challenging for parents and others. When, for example, a teenager who is taller and outweighs her parents is aggressively refusing to take on her responsibilities, it can be very difficult for the parents to maintain their boundaries around their parental responsibilities. But it is important for parents to bear in mind that any person – child or adult – who exhibits threatening words or actions is attempting to draw attention to unexpressed hurts within, and is not consciously trying to hurt others. This truth can be hard to take on board, particularly in the face of seriously troubled behaviours, such as property destruction or beating up an old person or knife assault. Teenagers who 'act-out' in such troubling ways are extremely unlikely to have experienced enduring unconditional love in their holding worlds; indeed this may well be the very loss they are attempting to bring to light. Parents can often come into their parental role with a considerable amount of unresolved emotional vulnerability from their own childhoods and are not in a position to provide the crucial foundation of unconditional love for their children. Such parents need the kind of help and support that focuses not just on how to respond effectively to teenagers' troublesome behaviours, but also on how to deal with their own inner insecurities and fears.

Troublesome behaviour comes from inner turmoil

Parents need to understand that how individuals – adults and children – view themselves influences everything they do, think, say and feel. As described in Chapter 6, how an individual feels about herself may be close to the truth of her unconditional worth and lovability – reflected in high self-esteem – or she may be far from consciously knowing the truth of her self and be operating from a screen or shadow self – reflected in low self-esteem.

When, in childhood, a person does not receive the safe holding of unconditional love, she develops a screen or shadow self to protect and to offset further threats to her presence. In most cases, infants are close to their true self, they are close to their unconditional worth; this is reflected in their spontaneity, their affection, their ability to receive love, their confidence, their love of learning, their curiosity and their ability to make their needs known. Furthermore, success and failure have no effect on them, they trip, they fall, they succeed but, no matter the outcome of their actions, they progress onto the next challenge. Tragically, many children, adolescents and adults have travelled a long, long distance from that original place of sureness of their unconditional worth and lovability. It is not that parents, and other significant adults in children's lives, want deliberately to push children into hiding their real self, but they themselves are in hiding and operate from their own shadow selves that do not reflect the solidity of their own uniqueness, individuality and sacredness.

Children wisely find ways of managing in the face of parents' defensive behaviours. Some children conform to the shadow behaviours of parents and others; such conformity brings the comfort of feeling less threatened and attaining some kind of acceptance but because the acceptance is conditional on certain behaviours, it never truly reaches the hearts of children. Rather than conforming, some teenagers rebel against the shadow behaviours of their parents and others, but this too is a case of shadow begetting shadow, leading to deeper darkness in relationships. The aim of rebellion is to counter-control, but the behaviours that are threatening to those who rebel are the very ones they themselves are using to reduce hurt. These teenagers are not free but are imprisoned by the attempts to offset further blows to their sense of self. Whether teenagers conform or rebel, insecurity blocks their mature progress until such time as opportunities arise for them to free themselves of living in shadowlands. There is a very important opportunity for progress when their parents or other significant adults come into their own enlightened presence.

Some shadow behaviours of adults
Some examples of shadow behaviours displayed by parents and other adults that impel young people into hiding are:

- irritability
- dismissiveness
- aggression
- passivity
- unrealistic expectations
- apathy
- over-protection
- lack of affection
- violence
- dominance
- rigidity
- perfectionism
- fear of failure
- addiction to work
- addiction to success
- advice-giving
- anxiety
- depression.

The frequency, intensity and endurance over time of these behaviours are telling factors in assessing how shadowed the parents themselves are and, in turn, how shadowed their children have needed to be. Parents who engage in any of the above listed behaviours deserve compassion, not judgement – because judgement only propels people into stronger defensive behaviours, whereas compassion may provide the first stepping stone towards redemption of their true selves.

Some shadow behaviours of teenagers
The shadow responses exhibited by teenagers can be of either a *transient*

or *enduring* nature. The transient responses arise largely around the new challenges that adolescence brings – for example, acceptance by peer group, physical and sexual development, experience of sexual attraction, increased academic competitiveness, greater educational responsibilities, and school examinations that have a determining influence on their future educational and career prospects. Examples of transient defensive reactions include:

- worrying about having a pleasing personality
- examination anxiety
- concern about physical appearance
- wanting to be liked
- 'hard man' behaviour
- not liking their bodies or how they look
- shyness
- rebelliousness
- anxiety about not having enough money
- sexual insecurity.

Enduring shadow behaviours have their roots in much earlier life. Some examples of enduring shadow behaviours exhibited by a high percentage of teenagers include:

- perfectionism
- intense worry about examinations
- wanting to drop out of school
- having no friends
- feeling unattractive
- hating themselves
- pessimism and fatalism
- feeling that they are never good enough
- avoiding contact with their peers
- intense shyness
- having a strong feeling that nobody likes them
- having a terror of failure
- isolating themselves
- sexual promiscuity
- depression
- high anxiety

- suicidal feelings and thoughts
- aggression
- refusal to listen or accept help
- self-harming.

In the case of transient shadow responses, parents can be assured that further life experience will more than likely resolve these uncertainties for their adolescent offspring. However, the more enduring and intense defensive behaviours are a cause for serious concern. Sadly, when parents themselves act out from a dark inner world, they are not in a position to see that help is needed to resolve the deep insecurities that darken the family. Denial, blaming of others, covering up the problems are all too common responses and, sometimes, it takes a tragedy before help is sought.

Responding to teenage turmoil

George Bernard Shaw, the Irish playwright, said, 'You can't cure a problem by hurting.' In the same vein of thought, the Buddha taught that: 'Hate cannot be conquered by hate; only love can conquer hate.' When young people manifest their inner turmoil through troubling behaviours, such as self-harming, attempting to take their own lives, drinking excessively, driving dangerously or being verbally aggressive, then any form of critical, judgemental or punishing *reactions* will only add fuel to the fire of hurt that they are already experiencing. Neither do reactions, such as patronising, moralising, preaching, advising or reassuring, help young people when they are in inner turmoil. It is understandable that when teenagers are in turmoil, their parents may find themselves under siege. It often happens, for example, that parents blame themselves, which throws them into considerable turmoil; such a reaction means that they are not in a solid place to respond constructively to whatever is troubling their son or daughter. Reactions, such as 'look what you're doing to your mother' or 'you've really let us and yourself down' or 'aren't you ashamed of yourself?' or 'what a sorry mess you've got yourself into', are reflective of the troubled inner worlds of the adults who respond in these ways and only serve to create further threat in the lives of young people.

The loving response to troubling behaviour, whether acting-in or acting-out – the latter often being experienced by adults as more troublesome than the former but both being equally expressive of turmoil within the young person – is to recognise its underlying intention; this being to show others the past and present hurts being experienced and to get some form of attention. Adults need to understand that in a situation where loving kindness is not the emotional diet of the day, any form of contact – even if it is heartbreakingly punishing – will be sought. Finding such a loving response can present a huge challenge to parents and other adults in the young person's life because they themselves have not experienced such loving responsiveness to their troubling behaviours – either in the past as children or in present adult life.

Parents often tell us that they find themselves repeating the very hurtful parenting experiences that they themselves had as children. We have heard parents say, for example, 'I'm sounding just like my mother' or 'I couldn't believe it when I found myself reacting to my daughter in the same hypercritical way father responded to me'. These parents, in their reactions are, like young people, attempting to draw attention to their own unresolved hurts, either by acting-out (for example, blaming, criticising, pushing and hitting) or by acting-in (for example, withdrawing, not talking for weeks on end, blaming themselves and ignoring what is going on). Adults, when they have not reflected on the reasons why they act in the ways they do, are in just as much need of understanding, support and help as are young people in order to resolve the hurts that lie behind their defensive reactions. But unless adults take on the responsibility of resolving the childhood neglects they have themselves experienced in their homes, schools and communities, it is unlikely that they will be able to respond maturely to young people's expressions of inner turmoil. In light of the statistics quoted at the start of this chapter, the responsibility of self-reflection among the significant adults in the lives of young people is particularly urgent. Adults (for example, parents, family members, teachers, psychologists, counsellors, psychotherapists, medical doctors, psychiatrists, social workers) can only support young people to come to the same level of maturity that they themselves have achieved.

Separateness is a second dimension of loving responsiveness to troubling behaviours. Progress in resolving young people's distress requires parents and other significant adults to find the kind of separateness from the presenting troubling behaviours that leads to proaction rather than reaction. The parent who stays separate does not personalise the troubling behaviour but knows that it is always about the teenager who exhibits it and that it is not intended as a rejection of others. In proaction, there is a compassionate and genuine attempt to understand what lies behind the difficult behaviours so that the focus can be on the support and resources needed to resolve the inner distress. While inner turmoil mostly arises from how young people see themselves and how they feel they are seen by significant others – many young people complain, for example, of feeling unloved, 'a failure', 'the black sheep', or 'a burden' to their parents – it is important not to make assumptions about what is going on for young people, but instead to provide the support, love and patience and active listening that will enable them to name their troubles themselves, so that the real issues that need to be resolved come to the surface.

Take the case of the widowed father worried about his teenage daughter's glue-sniffing. The father assumed that his daughter's glue-sniffing was caused by her guilt of surviving the car crash in which her mother had died. However, it emerged in therapy with the young person that the glue-sniffing was triggered by feeling emotionally suffocated by her father since her mother's death – the father had transferred his dependence on his deceased wife onto his daughter and had become over-involved in her life. For the girl, at this stage of her life, there were important needs relating to her separating out from her parent, becoming independent and developing relationships outside the family as preparation for leave-taking. These needs were being blocked in her relationship with her father; her glue-sniffing metaphorically represented the experience of her father being 'glued' to her and the difficulty for her of challenging her father 'to get a life' of his own. Her father did take on board the underlying intention of his daughter's troubling behaviours and came for therapy himself to resolve his tendency to create co-dependent relationships. The daughter was relieved of the responsibility for her father's wellbeing and now had the safety to separate out from him and have a life of her own.

Turmoil arising from experiences of rejection

The experience of being 'turned down' by someone to whom you are attracted is common in the teenage years, when young people are exploring attraction and relationships. For a teenager – as indeed for any one – the ending of a relationship or being 'turned down' by another can be a very difficult time. While the parents of the teenager may understand that the other young person's rejecting behaviour is 100 per cent about that young person, it is unlikely that the teenager herself, in the throes of bitter disappointment and hurt, will be able to take on board the advice of 'don't take it personally'. The teenager deeply upset following the loss of an existing or potential relationship does not need advice but does need comforting, support, holding and listening. It is only when the sandstorm of hurt, disappointment and anger has settled down that is it likely the teenager will be in a position to understand her reactions.

Sadly, following 'a let down' some young people, in their fear of recurrences of rejection, withdraw from any further relationship risk-taking. In order to avoid the very sad prospect of not being able to reach out for love, teenagers need to be helped to accept and understand the experience of 'rejection' and to discover ways of accommodating it within a loving acceptance of themselves. In taking on this challenge, the teenager will go a long way towards finding independence, self-knowledge and self-understanding and a sense of abiding security and adventure, regardless of her relationship status. Furthermore, if teenagers can be supported and encouraged to embrace the reality that there will always be challenges in life in reaching their goals and dreams, they will begin to see that experiences of 'rejection' offer opportunities to come into their fullness as a unique human being.

Dealing with 'rejection' is essentially about dealing with how one feels and thinks about your self. The more a teenager is in possession of her own individuality and unique sense of self, the less she will personalise the actions of another – whether these actions be joyful or disappointing. Once through the initial highly emotional aftermath, teenagers may be ready to accept that their reaction to being 'let down' by another is a mirror of their own poor sense of themselves and their projection of 'mend my life' or 'make me happy' onto the other person is what they need to do for themselves, but which they are afraid to do. When there is dependence for your happiness on another, it becomes very difficult not to personalise what is perceived as rejection, but the experience of feelings of rejection are the opportunity to come into love and acceptance of yourself and independence. People are naturally attracted to sureness and self-possession and if a teenager can accept a 'no' response gracefully and hold on to her own sense of worth and dignity, chances are the next time she takes a relationship-risk, the response will be positive.

Parents may well ask, 'How can a 'no' from another person be about that other person?' There are many reasons why one young person may not respond to another teenager's overtures. It may be that the rejecting person is afraid of commitment or, subconsciously, that the teenager being 'rejected' is a reminder of a parent who is controlling or passive, or it could be that the young person is not interested in a relationship, or may be still hurting from a previous relationship, or it may be that school studies are the priority. It may be that rejected teenager does not fit with the other person's 'dream' in the same way that there are many young people who do not fit with the rejected teenager's particular 'dream'.

It is the mark of maturity to be honest and appreciate honesty in return. The last thing any teenager needs is to pursue a relationship with somebody who does not really want to be in the relationship but has not got the courage to say so. When a teenager encounters a refusal, it is an act of independence to show appreciation and respect for that decision by no longer pursuing that person. It helps if the young person can learn to read the signs and signals of the other, and can pay heed to the body language as well as listening to the spoken word, and when one contradicts the other to take cues from the body language as it rarely lies. Most importantly, the teenager needs to hold on to her own sense of self.

CHAPTER ELEVEN

What most alarms: Teenage addictions

- Addictive responses
- Addiction to success
- Addiction to what others think
- Addiction to being in control
- Addiction to substances

Addictive responses

We emphasise again here the need to understand that there is a unique story behind all troubling behaviours. It needs to be borne in mind that the inner turmoil being signalled by the outer behaviours is unique to each teenager exhibiting the behaviours, and calls out for unique responsiveness from parents and any other adults involved. Keeping this very much in mind, this chapter examines four addictions often exhibited in the teenage years. Whilst most parents recognise addictions to a substance as a cause for concern, there are what can be called *process addictions* that are equally telling of blocks to the young person's progress and wellbeing. The three process addictions focused on are: success, approval from others and being in control.

All addictions have one main purpose and that is to fill the inner void a person has, arising from not having managed to attract a parent or other significant adults by his or her unique, sacred and creative presence. When what is real has not worked, we cleverly find a substitute – for example, success, pleasing or controlling. But there is no rest for those who are addicted, because you are only as good as your last success or pleasing of another or controlling of another. There is the enduring fear that next time the substitute behaviour may not work.

Addiction to success

Addiction to success is very common in our society and, no doubt, is implicated in some of the suicide and self-harming behaviours exhibited among young people. Alarmingly, suicide among young people is on the rise. Whether it is a child, adolescent or adult who takes his own life because of a failure to succeed, every one of us needs to sit up and ask the question: What kind of societal holding world are we creating whereby any person can believe they are worthless when they fail to make the high grade?

Take the case of the mother distraught because her daughter who was studying medicine had for the first time in her academic life failed an examination. The daughter felt her life was over, was feeling deeply depressed and suicidal, had stopped eating and was not sleeping. She was refusing too to return to university. The response to the mother's question, 'Can you help my daughter?', was that her daughter would free herself of her addiction to success once helped to come to a place where she could strongly assert, 'I'm not an examination result.' The tragedy is when a parent – or other significant adult such as a teacher – confuses the person with academic performance. When the young person intuitively knows that she is no longer attracting her parents by her amazing and unique presence, darkness descends on her interior world and academic success becomes the substitute way of gaining some light of approval and recognition. But the problem with the addiction to success is that she knows she is only as good as her last success and is terrified that the next time she may not succeed. Failure in an examination confirms her worst fears – her protective strategy has failed.

When a young person is emotionally devastated by an examination failure, a much more serious examination is required of what has brought the person to such a dependent place and such a confusion of himself with success. When the parents of the young person are equally devastated, then an examination of the ethos of the family is necessary; this involves the major challenge of both parents examining their own level of maturity and the quality of the relationship that each has with the teenager who is traumatised. It is frequently the case that a parent has an addiction to success that is more seriously and deeply rooted than that of a son or daughter. In the case of the medical student mentioned above, her mother asked several times, 'How soon will you have my daughter back to university?' A mother who loves her daughter unconditionally for her true self would have asked the question, 'How soon can you return my daughter to a place of wellbeing?' The mother's question reveals her own insecurities and vulnerabilities that, of course, are equally deserving of compassion and responsiveness.

The person who is addicted to success is trying to flag that he is greatly impeded from getting on with his life. The student who is mature and operates from an inner stronghold of self may well be disappointed with a particular examination result, but he will not be devastated; he will be able to acknowledge his disappointment but will embrace the disappointing result as an opportunity from which to learn and progress. The difference between the person who loves to learn and the person who is success-driven is that the former views learning as an adventure, while the latter sees it as a strain, a worry, a pressure. The person who is addicted will also be highly competitive, whereas the person who loves learning will be competitive with himself; this being the healthiest form of competition.

Success addiction does not add to the security, development, productivity and creativity of a society but, on the contrary, takes a huge toll on the wellbeing of the individual himself and on all others who live, study and work with this 'driven-ness'. Parents and educators have an urgent responsibility to restore a love of learning to classrooms/lecture rooms and, most of all, to restore a love of person to family and educational holding worlds.

Addiction to what others think

Even more common than the addiction to success is the addiction to the approval of others. This addiction can be particularly acute for teenagers. The questions below provide some index of the existence of a craving for approval or acknowledgement

- Does the teenager constantly ask for approval with questions such as: 'Did I do a good job?' or 'How do I look?', and then find he is disappointed by the reply?
- Does the teenager have difficulty in saying 'no' to other people's requests?
- Does the young person demand affection from others and, when not given, feel hurt and let down?

- Does the teenager seem inwardly resentful when somebody fails to acknowledge a kindness or favour done?
- Does the teenager have a 'need to be needed' or a 'need to be liked?'
- Does the teenager conform to the wishes of others without consideration of his own likes?
- Does the teenager seem to feel 'everything is my fault' and then spend time feeling guilty?
- Does the young person express worry about what others think following meeting them?

The need for approval dates back to childhood when the child cleverly tries to find ways to please the significant people in his life – those on whom he depends for his survival. The drive for approval arises in a family, or classroom or other significant holding world, where there is constant disapproval, lack of encouragement, affection and warmth, and a lack of belief in the child. It is devastating for children when their natural ways of gaining recognition do not work – their smile, raising their arms to be picked up, their humour, their tenderness, their excitement and eagerness, their responsiveness to being nurtured, their expressiveness, spontaneity and adventuresomeness, and their difference and individuality. The emergence of an addiction to approval indicates that conformity to the ways of an important person is being demanded and woe betide the child who does not dutifully respond. For example, a parent or teacher who is dominant, and believes he is always right, will demand and command acquiescence to his beliefs and ways of behaving. The child in this situation ingeniously develops an addiction to what this adult thinks, says and does because he knows the dangers of harsh abandonment if he does not conform. The wisdom in being addicted to the approval of others is that it enables the young person to anticipate what is wanted of him and thereby reduces the possibility of rejection and the accompanying overwhelming hurt and darkness. In a holding world that is over-controlling and demanding, it is essential for children's survival that they find a substitute way of gaining approval, and worrying and watching out for what adults think, say and do is one such powerful strategy. But there is no substitute for the real thing of unconditional recognition, and teenagers who continue to be addicted to the approval of others are in constant fear of not identifying the demands of the adults or peers they fear most in their holding worlds. There is no security, no peace, no relief, no contentment and no real love – just a way of trying to avoid occurrences of rejection and hurt.

Whilst children, out of dependence, necessarily and wisely develop an addiction to what others think and say, teenagers with the support of parents, and other significant others, can be enabled to separate out from dependence on others, to become their own person and to live their own life and not the life of others. Teenagers need to be given safety to use their precious energy and creativity not in seeking external approval but in serving their progress in living. This safety comes from the young person developing the ability to value and approve of himself and to stand on his own two capable feet. Rather than giving his power away and being victim to others' approval, he can enjoy creating a life for himself, and reclaim his right to live his own unique and individual life. Where the addiction to approval is deep-seated, considerable support and sometimes professional psychotherapeutic help is needed for the teenager to be safe to cut the ties that have bound him. It is likely that similar responses will be needed for the teenager's parents, who themselves are probably also heavily addicted to the approval of others. When parents themselves seek help, it paves the road for the young person to also seek resolution of this process addiction.

Addiction to being in control

The addiction to being in control can manifest itself in different forms in a teenager's life. For example, the addiction to being in control can be expressed in the drive to be thin, to be the 'perfect' weight and shape. The overwhelming need to be in control can also be expressed in a phobia of flying; in the mind of the person with this phobia, being in an aeroplane 30,000 feet above the ground, in a situation where they have absolutely no control over what happens, is a bridge too far.

If the addiction to the approval of others is a substitute means of gaining recognition and avoiding rejection, the drive to be in control is also a substitute means of holding on to others and ensuring that they do not become a source of emotional threat. The addiction to control arises from fear of the unknown, of the unexpected or of being controlled by another. The experience of un-safety for the expression of spontaneous individuality is the hidden truth that lies behind the defensive ways of those who are addicted to being in control. The following questions provide some index of the existence of a compulsion to be in control:

- Does the young person tend to dominate a conversation and resent any person who interrupts?
- Does the young person tell others what to say, think and do, and disapprove strongly if they decline his advice?
- Does the young person organise his life so that he knows exactly how things turn out? Does he panic when the unpredictable and unexpected turn up?
- Does the young person tend to think everything out before taking a risk?
- Once the young person has expressed a view or position on something, does he rigidly stick to his position when challenged?
- Does the young person believe that if it were not for the actions of others (parents, siblings, peers) life would work much better?
- Does the young person tend to make meticulous plans or endless to-do lists?
- Does the young person fear change?

Trying to establish control is a clever attempt to offset fear of the unexpected. For those teenagers in whose early lives there were considerable experiences of the unexpected and unpredictable, the drive to be in control emerges as being understandable and wise, since predictability and consistency are fundamental to the creation of safety in the holding worlds of family and school. The compulsion to be in control may also develop in protective response to significant adults who themselves over-control. The child exposed to over-control becomes the teenager who is a 'control freak' so that he offsets control by another. This teenager always has his focus on the other and on the outside world and not on himself. With this young person you dare not contradict, disagree, criticise or attempt to show any difference. Insecurity has led to the clever strategy of terrifying others, so that they dare not abandon him. Although the teenager never feels seen and loved for his unique self, the substitute recognition reaped from control is better than anonymity.

The hallmarks of individuals who control are rigidity and tension. The provision of support to trust themselves to take care of themselves, no matter what comes their way, is one powerful way of enabling young people to let go of the need to control. These teenagers need opportunities to experiment with their spontaneity and sense of play and fun, and to seek out individuals who display these real ways of being. When a young person's need to be in control is intense and enduring, it is advisable to seek professional psychotherapeutic help to alleviate the inner sense of helplessness and, sometimes, hopelessness that is likely being experienced. Once again, the first step is for the parents to look to their own behaviours and to examine the degree to which they themselves may be over-exercising control in the family holding world. Resolution of their own inner insecurities is a prerequisite to helping their teenage son or daughter.

Addiction to substances

The addictions that tend to be most familiar, and most alarming, to parents are those to substances – alcohol, drugs, food and nicotine. The underlying psychological processes are the same for addiction to substances as for any other addictions – all addictions are a protective strategy in the face of threat in the addict's important holding worlds. It can be seen how these substances also serve as substitutes for the void within when unconditional love is absent. Alcohol, for example, can give a teenager a warm, full, heady, 'out of it' feeling. Food can be 'sweet', filling, comforting and immediately gratifying. Drugs can have the effect of creating a numbing, floating and 'beyond it all' feeling, or the effect of intensifying feeling or creating a sense that 'everything is all right'. The wisdom in the compulsion to take these substances is that they bring a substitute fullness, albeit temporary, that, tragically, spontaneous reaching out when a child did not achieve. But the void the teenager attempts to fill is bottomless, and once the effects of the particular substance have worn off, the raw feeling of emptiness – of abandonment – rises again, and he is plunged back into the cycle of addictive behaviour. Young people caught in the addictive cycle need high levels of support – and almost always professional help – to find the safety to risk again the real way of finding fulfilment, through unconditional love and regard for themselves. This is a major challenge not only for the young person himself but for others in his life.

All addictions affect relationships with others. Indeed, sometimes the nature of the relationships created by the young person is a mirror of the earlier neglectful relationships he has experienced from childhood – the having to prove himself, the having to please and the having to control so that the unexpected does not happen. The effects of substance addictions have more evident effects on relationships, particularly addictions to alcohol, drugs and food. The typical situation is that the addiction rules the roost and anybody who challenges the effects of the addictive behaviours on the family, and on the wellbeing of the young person who is addicted, is in emotional, and sometimes physical, peril. The young person can react with hostility and aggression or withdrawal into silent hostility that can go on for weeks on end, and often there is an escalation of the addictive behaviours.

The teenager who is addicted is terrified of losing the substitute way of feeling 'fulfilled' and will not let go of his addiction easily. When the parent, or other adult in a helping role, remains steadfast in the resolve to no longer tolerate the effects of the addictive behaviours, the teenager who is addicted may be more disposed to accept help for the addiction. The nature of the help received is a critical issue. Helping agencies or professional individuals who see the addiction to the substance as the problem may well try to get the young person to stop taking the particular substance, but for whose good? Certainly, other people affected by the addictive behaviours may experience relief, but the underlying meaning and intention, and psychological rightness, of the addictive responses have not been acknowledged and taken into account. In any case, what frequently emerges is 'symptom substitution' whereby the teenager develops an alternative, less relationship-threatening, addiction; for example, shifting from addiction to alcohol to heavy reliance on tranquilisers or addiction to attendance at peer group meetings or to excessive exercise. Whatever new addiction is created, it has the same purpose as the original addiction – to fill the inner void.

There is no intention here to minimise the effects of addictions on significant others in the young person's life, but resolution does not lie in tackling head on the outer addictive behaviours. Interventions need to be of a nature that acknowledges that the addiction is not itself the problem but rather a creative response to an early problem in life – experiences of abandonment – and that understands that resolution lies in the creation of unconditionally loving relationships. The relationship between the person helping and the teenager seeking help needs to be of an unconditional loving nature so that the early abandonment experiences begin to be addressed in the present relationship.

In the safe holding world of unconditional love, empathy, understanding and realness, the young person gradually has the chance to realise his true worth and value and to begin to live out from that inner stronghold of self.

CHAPTER TWELVE

What most alarms: Teenage psychiatric labels

- Teenage psychiatric labels
- Attention deficit and hyperactivity 'disorders'
- Teenage 'schizophrenia'
- Oppositional defiance 'disorder'
- Anti-social behaviour

Teenage psychiatric labels

In our society, teenagers in distress and who manifest that distress in extreme 'acting-out' behaviours are likely to be labelled as suffering from one of the disorders listed below:

- attention deficit disorder (ADD)
- attention deficit with hyperactivity disorder (ADHD)
- oppositional defiance disorder (ODD)
- teenage schizophrenia
- anti-social behaviour.

It is understandable that parents can feel frightened and confused if their teenager exhibits troubled behaviours that seem extreme. Different professionals operate from different models in their approach to such behaviours. The psychiatric model views troubled behaviours as 'disorders' that have their source in biochemical, neurological or genetic factors, and treatment mainly focuses on medication. The psychosocial model views troubled behaviours not as 'disorders', but as responses to the nature of the relationship worlds in which the teenagers find themselves. In this latter model, rather than 'treatment', the professional considers responsiveness to the significant factors that emerge in hearing the person's life story. The psychiatric and psychosocial models are very different in approach, but it is important for parents to know that they have a choice, to inform themselves as best they can and to make their own decisions based on their own considerations.

What follows is an attempt to show that there is purpose and wisdom to each one of these 'disorders'; to show that they are, in fact, wise and creative manifestations of inner turmoil, and that, when they are understood in this way, there is hope for resolution, if also great challenge for everyone involved.

Attention deficit and hyperactivity 'disorders'

In recent decades, many Irish teenagers have been labelled as having attention deficit disorder (ADD) or attention deficit disorder with hyperactivity (ADHD) and whilst schools do their best to provide special needs and support teachers, parents can find themselves at their wits' end about how best to respond.

Our own experience of children and teenagers who manifest inattentiveness and/or hyperactivity or oppositional defiant behaviour is that these are wise creations in unsafe holding worlds in which the child has few options available to her. Of course, these creations pose a challenge to adults, and parents and teachers in particular need support and help to understand and respond effectively to children's expressions of distress and to ensure their wellbeing is safeguarded. The more adults recognise that children possess the most amazing natural ways of attracting us to their individual, unique and lovable presence, the more they will understand that, when these real ways do not work, children subconsciously create substitute ways of drawing attention to their presence and these ways continue into the teenage years and later into adulthood. The less successful are the natural, real ways of attracting, the stronger the substitute responses need to be. It is noteworthy that it is the children who 'act-out' who are most likely to be labelled, whilst the children who 'act-in' have no labels attached to their creations. Children who 'act-in' – the ' goodie-good' child, the 'perfectionist', the 'ever-so-pleasing' child, the success-addicted child – are not labelled because they do not disturb the lives of adults, but the sad fact is that they too are distressed within themselves and often are more at risk than those children who 'act-out'.

Whether a teenager 'acts-out' or 'acts-in', it is essential that the key holding worlds of the young person – home, school, community – are examined and that the helping responses arise from that informed place. Parents and teachers, out of their fear of being judged 'bad', can become defensive when such an examination of holding worlds is proposed. There is no doubt that both parenting and teaching are among the most difficult of professions and that society has let down both professions in terms of adequate preparation and training for their responsible roles. There is also no doubt that parents and teachers always do their best, but the reality is that their own unresolved insecurities and early-life conflicts impact on the lives of children. The three-fold challenge for the significant adults in the teenager's life is for them to get to know their own selves, get to know the young person and let the young person get to know them. The outward signs of turmoil may be similar across millions of children but the inner and outer turmoil being experienced is peculiar to the individual teenager and that teenager's particular life story and life circumstances.

The importance of considering choices other than labelling and medication is strongly argued by Timimi and Radcliffe (2005). According to these authors 'children quickly become objects' of such descriptions as ADHD, 'Their creativity, capacity for 'exceptional behaviours' and diversity go unnoticed.' Furthermore, the label of ADHD adversely affects parents, teachers and others caring for young people by 'causing them self-doubt about their capacity to teach and provide care'. These authors also say that the opportunities for developing reflexive, appreciative child management practices and skills are lost and 'the chance to build a repertoire of therapeutic skills and practices that might facilitate people to talk about their experience in ways that can create more empowering meanings that build on their own knowledge is also lost'.

Teenage 'schizophrenia'

Understandably, it can be extremely distressing for parents to witness a teenage son or daughter engaging in the kind of paranoid or delusional or hallucinatory behaviour labelled 'schizophrenic' and, not surprisingly, their response is often one of panic. One approach to such behaviours is to see them as being due to biochemical imbalances or genetic factors, and then the treatment of choice is medication. However, it is wise for parents to know that this is not the only approach and that there is debate about its effectiveness. For example, Bentall (2009), a clinical and research psychologist, using sophisticated research techniques, has concluded that there is no evidence to support either a biochemical or genetic source for these disturbing responses and his conclusions are borne out by others (see, for example, Whitaker, 2010).

Another approach is to consider environmental factors. There is considerable evidence that factors such as early childhood traumatic influences and sustained stress are linked to particular syndromes. An alternative to mediation is psychotherapy which, according to Bentall, numerous studies have shown is 'remarkably effective'. Whilst psychotherapy works, the research raises some interesting issues: no evidence has been found that any one type of psychotherapy is more effective than any other, but there is evidence that psychotherapists are most effective when they are carrying out a type of therapy in which they strongly believe and to which they are committed. Another finding is that the effectiveness of psychotherapy is connected to the ability of the therapist to form a *therapeutic alliance* with the person seeking help. This is usually described as an 'affectional' bond between the person who is distressed and the psychotherapist and their ability to work together towards mutually agreed goals. In our own work, we regard psychotherapy as a *co-creation* that involves both the creativity of the therapist and that of the person seeking to understand and resolve her troubled state.

In our view, there is no mystery about why an affectional, co-creational relationship is critical to positive therapeutic outcomes, as the sources of distress always lie in relationships, particularly earlier relationships with parents and other significant adults in the person's life. Biography – the story of the person's relationships – is central to understanding the person's distress. If the sources of inner and outer conflict lie in troubled relationships, surely it makes sense that the resolution lies in benign, loving relationships, most especially in the relationship between the person who is disturbed and the care professional. Ultimately, the deeper purpose of the person-therapist relationship is that through holding, which is unconditional, empathic and genuine, the person in distress finds the safety to come to a place of love and responsibility for her self and her actions. Depending on the level of distress experienced, this therapeutic relationship may be short lived or long lived. Great patience is required on the part of the care professional because when a person has been deeply hurt, she will take a long time to trust being loved by others and loving herself.

There is nothing simplistic about the notion that the therapeutic relationship created with individuals in distress is the critical factor in their recovery, but there is certainly a profound simplicity to it. However, what is profound is not that easily attained; indeed it is 'rocket science' to create an effective therapeutic relationship. In the effective therapeutic relationship, the professional helper needs to be dependably real in order to create the emotional safety for the other person to be transparently real, she needs to love the person unconditionally and be non-judgemental of whatever behaviour presents, she needs to draw out the creativity of the person's symptomatic responses, she needs to stay separate and not personalise the responses of the person in distress, she needs to be empathic and to communicate belief in the potential of the person. To effect the foregoing, the care professional needs to have gained a deep level of personal maturity.

Parents who experience a son or daughter exhibiting 'psychotic-type' behaviours of course want to ensure that their loved one gets the best possible help. Short-term medication may be required but medication, whilst it may reduce the symptoms, does not resolve the underlying emotional issues. Emotional issues call for a psychotherapeutic intervention. It would be wise also for the parents themselves – and, perhaps, other family members – to seek the help and support of a psychotherapist or a family therapist. When parents seek help themselves, it takes the spotlight off the young person who is highly distressed and shows their understanding that all parties in the network of relationships involved need to examine their own part in those relationships. Parents, through their own therapy, can also discover how best to respond to the teenager's troubling responses so that the young person's insecurities are not further exacerbated.

Oppositional defiance 'disorder'

Over the years, we have encountered individuals – both adults and young people – who when they are contradicted or are not getting a need met seemingly lose all control. Their reactions include shouting, swearing, wild and aggressive gesticulations, and sometimes violence. Always, they are verbally diminishing of the presence of the person who has not given in to their way. Teenagers who exhibit these behaviours tend to get the label of oppositional defiance 'disorder', but adults also display oppositional behaviours. For example, in workplaces employees can endure paroxysms of rage from a supervisor or employer who it appears 'cannot control himself'. Typical descriptions are 'he really loses it' or 'she just goes insane' and 'there's no talking to him' or 'she goes totally over the top', or 'he loses total control'.

To say that any one who exhibits these behaviours is 'out of control' is inaccurate. It is also inaccurate to say that they are suffering from a syndrome called oppositional defiance disorder. On the contrary, there is meaning and purpose to these behaviours and they have their source in early unsafe holding worlds. Far from being out of control, the person is desperately – if unconsciously – seeking to be in control. Rather than saying that the teenager is 'out of control' or 'gone over the top' or 'flipped her lid', it is far more accurate to say she is 'highly and aggressively controlling'. This individual has learned to use any weapons – physical, verbal and non-verbal – to gain what she has not gained through open and real ways of behaving. The oppositional behaviour has the effect of getting family members to tiptoe around her in their fear of sparking off another tirade. Little, if anything, is asked of this family member and she gets anything she wants. Sadly, passive responding by the other members of the family only serves to maintain the difficult behaviours and the deep insecurity of the young person.

The parent who does not actively take charge of care of her self in the face of a teenage son's or daughter's aggressively controlling behaviours is often in as much need of help as the teenager herself and is exhibiting a similar level of inner insecurity. The two extremes – one of passivity and the other of aggression – are both attempts at controlling the other. The person who employs passivity hopes to control the other person by not upsetting her and the person who 'acts-out' hopes to control through intimidation. When passivity meets oppositional defiance, no resolution is possible as nobody is taking charge of establishing definite and clear boundaries around respect for the self and the other, and around taking responsibility for meeting your own needs. Parents who are encountering a teenager who is 'ruling the roost' in the family will find guidance for effective responses to the situation in Chapter 7, which discussed the importance of boundaries. Where the situation has got out of hand, it is wise to seek professional support to re-establish boundaries.

Anti-social behaviour

Teenage anti-social behaviour needs to be understood as a response to the trauma of abandonment; trauma which may be temporary and insignificant or continuous and severe. It is a relatively straightforward task to respond to a teenager whose anti-social behaviour arises from a minor deprivation (for example, not allowed to go out to her friends) in a generally caring environment, but it is a very different matter when the adolescent has become anti-social as a defensive way of life. Extreme anti-social behaviour is always deep-rooted and becomes more frequent and complex the longer it continues without effective responsiveness. When a young person experiences overwhelming abandonment, the unconscious *intention* of her destructive behaviours is to *act-out* this intolerable state of abandonment; in the externalisation of her trauma, the hope is that somebody out there will contain or hold her in some way or other. When externalisation of her trauma does not gain her what she wants, she will escalate her destructiveness in a frantic attempt to find responsiveness.

Persistent delinquency signals a young person constantly on the edge of unbearable pain and despair. Her destructive behaviours offer some outlet, while challenging society – because the holding world of family has abandoned her – to impose the control that is not occurring in her home. At the extreme, acts such as stealing, drug dealing or violence, and consequent societal attempts to control, provide some attention to her seemingly impossible situation. This acting-out may become irresistible when there is little opportunity for more wholesome satisfaction. There is the additional factor that delinquent behaviours give her some sense of esteem from herself and her peers; it offers her a direction, even a career; and it can give her material goods through stealing or an emotional high through power over others. Because it has certain benefits and acts to mask despair and hopelessness of ever being loved, giving up anti-social behaviours may present as an unthinkable prospect for the young person involved. It is because of this that criminalising anti-social behaviours is unlikely to have any enduring impact.

At present there are three different responses to young people's anti-social behaviours:

- *reactive* response (which calls for incarceration and punishment)
- *management* response
- *treatment* response.

On its own, the first response repeats the anti-social behaviour of the young person and, accordingly, is unlikely to have any enduring impact. It is a case of 'treating like with like'.

Management involves the attempt to structure the environment in such a way that it responds to the intention of the anti-social behaviour of the young people in regard to their need for containment and safety. In mild cases, this can be enough to enable the young person's recovery of trust and emotional connection. But in more severe cases, where the teenager has been deeply hurt in personal relationships and is hugely wary of any emotional involvement, management needs to be more definite and structured to provide the necessary safe holding. Within a regimented environment, the young person who has endured severe deprivation may feel sufficiently secure to begin to experience a better quality of life. With a relaxation of control, the unbearable agony of not having being loved and cherished will erupt again, leading to renewed offending behaviour. This ensures distraction from the internal pressure and darkness and reinstates the call for the establishment of control from the outside. Management of anti-social behaviour through adventure camps where regimentation is the order of the day has been shown to be effective with young people who have offended. The maintenance of the strong holding environment may eventually lead to the young person being ready to pay attention to her chronic inner turmoil and her difficult life contexts.

Treatment of anti-social behaviour tends to be an intervention of much longer duration. Its aim is to help the young person to express outwardly in a real way her inner pain and to begin to be open to the receiving and giving of love. Where there are parents involved, this process needs to include them also as they, too, will need help to connect with themselves and with each other and with their son or daughter. The therapist in this situation would need to possess a very strong holding of self and a thorough knowledge of family dynamics, family therapy and psycho-therapy.

Whatever approach is taken to helping the young person resolve the deep emotional issues that lie behind her anti-social behaviours, sight must not be lost of the needs of those individuals whose wellbeing has been threatened by these behaviours. Their needs deserve as much recognition and positive responsiveness as the unmet needs of young people who display anti-social behaviours.

CHAPTER THIRTEEN

What most alarms: Teenage depression, shyness, self-harming, suicide attempts and suicide

- Persistent teenage inner turmoil
- Depression among teenagers
- Extreme shyness among teenagers
- Self-harming among teenagers
- Suicide and attempted suicide: The stark figures
- Attempted suicide: How parents can best respond

Persistent teenage inner turmoil

Many parents worry that a teenager who has become moody and withdrawn or verbally and physically aggressive may 'do something to themselves' and are often unsure what to do for fear of making matters worse. This chapter seeks to provide an understanding of the 'intentions' and wisdom underlying manifestations in young people of depression, extreme shyness, self-harming and suicidal behaviour. The chapter is particularly focused on the creation by parents of the physical, emotional and social safety required for young people to communicate directly and clearly what precisely it is that is deeply troubling them. The creation of safety is a deep and challenging process requiring persistence, understanding, compassion and patience.

Clearly, it is an easier undertaking when the attempts to create safety have been present from the beginning of the young person's life. But even if this has not been the case, it is never too late to pay heed when young people show through strong signals – such as depression – that they are experiencing severe threats in the holding worlds in which they participate. The young person moving into wider holding worlds – such as second or third-level education – inevitably encounters 'new' threats but troubling behaviours of the nature being discussed here inevitably arise from unresolved issues from childhood years; issues that persist into adolescence. Certainly there are deep self-esteem issues to be resolved and parents need strongly to examine their own level of self-esteem before embarking on helping their troubled sons or daughters; such inner journeying may be new to parents and they may need support and guidance for themselves in the process. It is important that parents and other adults understand that the most loving and helpful response they can offer the young person in turmoil is the commitment that they will undertake their own inner reflection. In this way adults will know from their own experience how difficult it can be to face into inner pain; they will recognise how they created their own substitute behaviours in the face of threat, and they will be aware of the fundamental human need to love and be loved unconditionally. Through accompanying themselves on the journey, they become fit guides to accompany the young people on their journey to peace and openness.

Depression among teenagers

It is important that both parents and teenagers make the distinction between moodiness and depression. The word 'depression' is often used loosely to describe commonly experienced feelings of sadness, disappointment, tiredness or just having 'a down day'. All of these feelings are apt responses to the 'ups' and 'downs' of adolescent life and are alerting the young people to the challenge to become more adult in how they deal with what life throws up for them. Moodiness in mid-to-late adolescence is a not uncommon response to the many challenges – physical, emotional, sexual, social and educational – that arise at this age and the fear of not being able to cope with such challenges. Certainly, young people exhibiting moodiness can be assured that experience and the support of family and friends will get them through these transient difficult times, but it is not wise to say to teenagers that 'time changes everything' because time per se changes nothing; only action changes how young people feel about themselves, the world and their future.

The duration of the feelings is an important factor distinguishing depression from feelings of sadness, disappointment or 'feeling down'.

Generally speaking, when depressive feelings persist for two weeks or more, then consultation with a professional is required, preferably somebody who is trained in psychotherapy and family dynamics – clinical psychologist, psychotherapist or family therapist. Depression is a revelation of emotional vulnerability that is much more serious than reaction to new challenges and verbal reassurances that 'this, too, will pass' or 'it's just a phase you're going through' or admonitions to 'snap out of it' do not help but instead pose further threat through lack of understanding and active listening.

In our experience of working with young people, the source of their depressive feelings lies with the repression or suppression of some or all aspects of their true nature; this suppression/repression having taken place out of fear of recurrence of experiences of rejection when these aspects of themselves had previously been shown spontaneously. The more qualities of their unique selves that teenagers have to hide, the deeper is the level of depression. It is important for parents, and other adults, to understand that depression is not an enemy, not an illness, but a cry from the human spirit, revealing the deep inner distress that needs to be resolved. When a teenager's depressive reactions are not detected and responded to compassionately by parents and significant others, then further substitute behaviours may emerge, such as addiction to drugs or alcohol, or self-harming, or suicidal feelings, or even suicidal actions.

Some of the possible signs of teenage depression that parents, teachers and other significant adults need to watch out for are:

- bouts of crying
- expression of feelings of emptiness inside
- a lack of enjoyment of activities that heretofore gave pleasure
- not going out with friends
- loss of appetite or overeating
- low energy
- suddenly not doing well in school
- brooding and unresponsive to requests
- suddenly and easily becoming anxious, irritable, violent or destructive
- describing life as hopeless and self as useless when things go wrong
- talking about death or suicide
- physically hurting him or her self.

The presence of any one of these symptoms is a cause for concern; the presence of several of them is cause for alarm and the need for urgent intervention.

The manner in which parents, teachers and other significant adults respond to the depressive feelings of teenagers can either facilitate or block the therapeutic process that is being called for. Responses – such as panic, advice-giving, labelling the depressive feelings as an illness, resorting to antidepressants as a first or only option, or trying desperately to 'find the reasons why', or blaming hereditary factors ('It's in your father's side of the family') – do nothing to ease the inner pain of the young person who is feeling depressed, but instead exacerbate the feeling of not being understood or really heard or seen.

What does help is to express concern and love, to create the safety for the young person to talk and to actively listen when he does talk. Confidentiality may be demanded by the teenager and, if so, this needs to be given unequivocally. If, later on, the adult involved has fears for the young person's safety, permission needs to be sought from the teenager to seek further support and help. If there is refusal (which is rare), the adult needs to communicate to the distressed teenager that out of love he cannot stand idly by and that it is too difficult to hold the knowledge on his own that the young person might hurt himself or attempt to take his own precious life. In taking this action, the adult needs to assure the young person that any other details of his life that have been revealed will be kept confidential, unless the young person instructs otherwise.

It is important that adults, and parents in particular, do not personalise the young person's depression and that they do not view it as a revelation that they have failed in their roles. Any such response is likely to deepen the young person's depression because there is distraction now onto the other's life and he may feel guilty and responsible for the visible signs of distress being shown by the parent. There are many reasons why a teenager may get depressed and even when the cause lies in family relationships, parents need to reassure themselves that they have done their best up to this time. Rather than seeing their son's or daughter's depression as a threat, it is mature to respond to it as an opportunity for relationships to deepen within the family. The need to stay separate, to not personalise, to not blame or judge themselves underlies how important it is for parents to undertake their own inner journey; parents need to have at least the beginnings of an inner stronghold if they are to be able to relate to the troubled young person in the manner needed.

Extreme shyness among teenagers

Parents can become very concerned when they see a teenage child being extremely shy and avoiding contact with peers and adults. 'Social phobia' – a term used to describe the situation where the person dreads being the focus of attention and will do anything to avoid such situations – occurs in all age groups and is a strong signal of underlying fears preventing spontaneous self-expression. Shyness is often part of the teenage experience; arising as a response to threats experienced in the wider holding worlds which they are now entering – threats experienced for example, around their 'attract-ability'. But as their sense of self becomes more solid, they begin to feel more confident and less threatened by social interactions. What is being flagged by extreme shyness is not transient fear of a 'new' threat but the exacerbation of fears that have been there from childhood.

There is a sizeable group of teenagers whose social fears arising in childhood persist into adulthood. Once the fear of public embarrassment takes hold, these teenagers feel powerless to think or reason their way out of panic; emotion is always stronger than reason. Their avoidance of social interaction is a very strong protector against the possible recurrences of earlier experiences of hurt around social self-expression, and they would need to have the reassurance that they can be there for themselves now before testing the waters of their present-life social world.

Some typical signs of social phobia are:
- blushing
- poor eye contact
- hunched posture
- stammering
- physical shaking
- heart palpitations
- stomach butterflies
- panic attacks
- avoidance of certain or all social events.

When asked why they dread socialising, teenagers suffering social phobia may give explanations such as the following:

- 'I can't stand being the centre of attention.'
- 'I don't know what to say to people.'
- 'I don't know what's expected of me.'
- 'I'm terrified of getting it wrong.'
- 'I'm afraid of being shown up.'
- 'I'm afraid I'll blush.'
- 'I'm afraid of fainting.'
- 'I'm afraid of making a fool of myself.'
- 'I'm afraid of being rejected.'
- 'I'm afraid of saying or doing the wrong thing.'
- 'I'm afraid people will see my hands shaking.'

Children are not born shy; on the contrary, babies and toddlers, generally, are open, spontaneous, curious and friendly. But children cleverly learn to develop shyness to offset further occurrences of humiliation, ridicule, criticism and rejection, if this is what they experienced when they were spontaneously expressive of themselves. What typically underlies social phobia is poor sense of self, dependence on others for approval and recognition and a conviction that whatever you do or say, you are going to be rejected outright.

The teenager's protection is to reject himself before others even have a chance of rejecting him.

The roots of social phobia inevitably lie in early experiences. It may be that the young person was rejected or humiliated when he displayed a behaviour that did not meet the approval of parents or some significant other – behaviours, such as clinging, crying, blushing, fainting, failing at something or showing stress. Or it may be that the child could not find a way of attracting a parent's interest or recognition and constantly felt overlooked, dismissed or unseen. Shyness then is not a problem but rather a protective strategy that defends against further hurt but that also flags the hidden unmet needs that are seeking to come into the light.

In helping teenagers who are shy, the focus needs to be on creating the emotional and social safety that enables them to take the risk again of expressing their unique presence and to become independent of the defensive behaviours of others; a risk that becomes possible as they begin to relate to themselves now with all the love, respect, recognition and visibility that they always deserved but did not receive. This kind of relationship with self becomes the all-powerful buffer needed in the face of defensive behaviours from others.

Essentially these teenagers who have been 'bitten' and are now several hundred times 'shy' need not to care anymore if they blush, shake, trip, fall, faint, fail, stammer; they need to understand for themselves that behaviour is just a way of experiencing the world and neither adds to nor detracts from their worth. Support and encouragement from parents is hugely important but what is even more important is that parents model social confidence and competence and be able to understand and resolve their own social fears. When such a process proves difficult either for the teenager or the parent, it is wise to seek psychosocial help.

Self-harming among teenagers

The term 'self-harming' is used to refer to acts such as cutting or burning self or overuse of medication. Self-harming is far more prevalent among female compared to male teenagers – a ratio of seven to one. Self-harming is a defensive strategy that is not uncommon in the teenage years: 12 per cent of the 15–17 year olds in the study by the National Suicide Research Foundation report that they had deliberately self-harmed, and, of this group, nearly 50 per cent report that they have self-harmed *more* than once. The two main reasons given are: 'I wanted relief from a terrible situation' and 'I wanted to die' (Sullivan et al., 2004).

It needs to be appreciated that factors such as family conflict, stress about school, relationship break-up between parents, problems with peers, bullying, sexual identity issues and low self-esteem are all significant contributors to self-harming. The intention of the physical wounding is to draw attention to the much deeper emotional wounding being experienced.

There is wisdom in self-harming in that hearts are touched when it is discovered that a teenager has been doing this to herself. It is very difficult to even imagine how a teenage girl can take a blade or a knife or a scalpel and cut into her own flesh, yet at some level adults can realise that there is some greater emotional pain present, and that the inducing of physical pain in some way reduces the emotional pain. Certainly the cuts and scratches powerfully *embody* the emotional cuts; the deeper the physical cuts, the deeper the emotional cuts. The self-harming represents an attempt to release some of the emotional pain, but there is the hope that some adult will spot her hidden turmoil without her having to draw direct attention to it herself; the scars are the flags of turmoil covertly flown.

In responding to self-harming behaviour, the quality of the teenager's family relationships is a crucial consideration as is the quality of the relationships with self, with teachers and with peers. Parents can experience great distress and bewilderment if they discover that their teenage son or daughter is self-harming. Not surprisingly, their reaction is often a mixture of panic, anger, sadness, confusion, blaming of oneself – 'Where have I gone wrong?' – and the impulse to control the teenager's self-harming. While all of these responses are understandable, they reflect the inner world of the particular parent experiencing them, and need to be recognised as a completely separate issue from the self-harming behaviour of the teenager; accordingly, it is important that parents first seek help for their own responses before embarking on helping their obviously highly distressed teenager. Parents always need to bear in mind that every human behaviour makes sense and, whilst it is very distressing to witness one's teenage child self-harming, it is vital not to judge, isolate, condemn or label but to set about understanding what has brought about such a symptom of inner turmoil.

Above all, it is important not to dismiss self-harming. The frequency, intensity and endurance of the self-harming incidents are important considerations in understanding the meaning of the self-harming behaviour. There are no general answers to why a teenager would self-harm – each teenager's reasons are unique and the parents' and any other professional helper's responses to the teenager's plight need to be uniquely tailored to the young person's particular life experiences. Parents can be reassured that psychotherapy or family therapy can lead to a resolution of the underlying unmet needs and hidden conflicts, but patience and persistence are necessary qualities as the process can sometimes be long.

Teenagers who self-harm often complain of hostility from professionals who find it difficult to cope with the repetitive nature of the behaviour and who perceive teenagers who self-harm as having no control over their actions. The tendency of these professionals is to label those who self-harm as 'mentally ill' and to employ treatments aimed at controlling the teenager's behaviour; the teenager may be given an ultimatum that the self-harming must stop in order to receive treatment. Such an approach is likely to prove counterproductive; denying people their primary coping mechanism is not effective because, if teenagers need to self-harm as a means of revealing and relieving their inner turmoil, they will find a way to continue but in a more secretive and perhaps more serious way. It is essential that the focus of therapy is on what lies hidden beneath the self-harming behaviours; it is the realisation and resolution of those hidden conflicts that gradually lead to a reduction or total cessation of the protective self-harming actions. Attempts to coerce young people into not physically hurting themselves – such as compulsory admission to a psychiatric hospital, medication without consent, unwanted continuous observation and the forcing of a contract of 'no self-harm' – can be seen as a violation of human rights. The 'good' intentions may well be there, but the intention does not produce the resolution; only 'good' action produces the real end needed. Furthermore, early childhood experiences of coercion may very well be the hidden turmoil underlying the self-harming behaviour.

The way forward is relationship – the forming of an unconditional, non-judgemental, non-possessive relationship with the teenager who self-harms. This can be a slow process and patience is essential because teenagers who have been seriously, deeply and repeatedly hurt will be slow to trust a relationship again. An understanding of the behaviour as meaningful is essential in creating the safe relationship that enables the unique hidden reasons for the self-harming to emerge into conscious awareness. The presence of love, compassion, understanding and belief in teenagers' capacity to resolve their fears and find more open and direct ways of living in this world will create the environment that enables healing and maturity.

Finally, it is useful for parents to bear in mind that many adults self-harm, in some way or other – for example, through rushing, severe dieting, excessive exercise, over-drinking, over-working, addictions to drugs or alcohol, perfectionism and obsessiveness – but these behaviours are often not identified as a self-harming defence. Such responses may not appear as dramatic and acute as cutting yourself, but they can also have devastating effects. Parents or other adults who wish to help teenagers to resolve their self-harming behaviours would be wise to set about identifying and resolving their own repertoire of self-harming responses at the same time. Teenagers are quick to spot double-standards and are not likely to respond to parents or other adults who engage with them in such defensive ways.

Suicide and attempted suicide: The stark figures

Research suggests that around 15 per cent of Irish teenagers contemplate suicide at some point in their young lives but, mercifully, only a small percentage of distressed young people attempt suicide. In Ireland in 2007, there were 413 recorded suicides, 47 of them under the age of 19 years. Sadly, children as young as 10 years (or less) are complaining of being depressed and of feeling suicidal and some are actually either attempting to take or are taking their own lives. A statistic that tends to be overlooked is that female young people are several times more likely to attempt suicide compared to their male peers. There is the danger that attempted suicide be seen as 'attention-seeking' behaviour and not taken seriously, but any suicide attempt is a serious sign of major inner conflict in the young person and it is vital that the signal is responded to with decisive caring. One of the possible reasons for the higher incidence of depression and suicide attempts among girls lies in our socialisation practices whereby girls, although they are encouraged to talk about their feelings, are not taught how to process and work with them and use them as a guide for action; in effect girls are given passive access to their feelings, but are left without the means to act upon them in an effective way and so are more likely to manifest their insecurities and fears in 'acting-in' ways, such as withdrawal, avoidance and depression. Boys, on the other hand, are denied access to their feelings and are more likely to mask their vulnerabilities behind 'acting-out' behaviours, such as verbal abuse, violence, fast driving, carelessness and 'bravado' behaviour.

The statistics are stark in themselves, but the torment they mask of those who have taken their lives is extreme as is the grief, turmoil and confusion that is experienced by family members left behind to deal with the tragedy and the loss. Death of a loved one at any time is an extremely painful and difficult experience but violent death can cause almost unbearable grief. Torment, guilt, loss of religious faith, despair, rage are but some of the reactions that parents, brothers and sisters and, indeed, close friends may undergo. The 'what if?', the 'why?', the 'what did I do wrong?' questions bombard the minds of loved ones left behind. The longing to see once more the loved one and to find the answers to the unanswerable questions can rage within. For somebody on the outside of the experience, it can be difficult to even imagine the depth, breadth and darkness of feelings the parents and other family members may be undergoing. The following poem, written by a friend whose son committed suicide, captures powerfully and articulately the aftermath of the suicide of a loved one and the responses from others that can bring comfort.

Please don't tell me you know how I feel
if all your children are alive.

Please don't tell me that time will help,
for me, time is now.

Please don't tell me that I'll get over it in time.
I'll never get over it – only learn to live with it.

Please don't give me pious platitudes such as
'It's God's will, he's an angel in heaven.'
I want my son here on earth.

Please don't avoid mentioning his name.
I need to talk about him.
Please don't tell me what I should or must do.
Only I know what I can do.

Please don't get uncomfortable with my tears.
I have little or no control over them.

Please don't be insulted when I don't converse.
I just don't have the energy for it.

Please don't tell me I'm looking much better today.
It's not the visible me that's in pain.

Please bear with me. I know you mean well.
But my grief is mine. I cannot share it.

Attempted suicide: How parents can best respond

While various media put the focus on the act of suicide as the problem, it is crucial that the spotlight is redirected onto the underlying turmoil being signalled by suicide and suicide attempts among young people. There is a responsibility on all adults charged with the care of children and teenagers to look deeply within their own hearts and examine the quality of the relationships between themselves and the young people manifesting distress. It is essential to try to uncover how the young person feels about him or her self, as it is this inner world of the self – which reflects the outer world of the relationships experienced by the teenager – that drives all behaviour. Ultimately, young people need the opportunities to tune into their feelings, to be able to recognise and identify them, to understand them as a very powerful ally – an ally who knows exactly how things are – and to learn how to use them to guide their actions, so they may resolve their inner turmoil and come to a place of peace with their own self and others.

In response to what appears to be a growing suicide rate among teenagers, there have been attempts to detect the signs of suicidal intentions. This can be very difficult because the person planning to take his own life may put on a 'brave' face in order not to be stopped from his planned course of action. Furthermore, when the young person sees an end in sight to his feelings of hopelessness and despair, he may experience feelings of relief. It needs to be also borne in mind that the nature of the inner turmoil leading to suicidal thoughts is peculiar to each person and will be signalled in particular ways by the particular person. However, there are some indicators of emotional pain and of the risk of the young person losing his already fragile hold on himself and on life. These possible indicators are concerned with what is happening *within* the person and what is happening *between* the teenager and significant others in his different holding worlds – in the family, in school, with friends, in the community. Manifestations from *within* the adolescent may take the form of frequent crying, agitation, physical and emotional withdrawal, personal neglect, persistent moodiness, loss of appetite, over-eating, over-drinking and avoidance of responsibilities. Other possible indicators are an overreliance on medication, staying in bed, absence from school and not wanting to meet friends. Signs that occur *between* the teenager and others may be expressions of feeling depressed and hopeless, verbalisations such as 'nothing is going to change', 'life is not worth living', 'prefer if I was dead', 'nobody cares', being seriously over-demanding, constant verbal repetition of feelings of depression, or obsession with a failed relationship. Of course, there are young people who manifest signs of depression, anxiety and despair and who do not attempt suicide, but these signs always need to be responded to with patience, love, understanding, support and the provision of hope. These caring responses can bring a person back from the edge of wanting to die. Sadly, it can also happen that due to unbearably black despair, the young person cannot internalise the love and concern shown and does take his own life. Ultimately, we cannot save another, but we can extend the loving support that enables the other to save himself.

A hard reality we are faced with in our society as a holding world is that young people can feel so invisible and so despise themselves that taking their own lives can present itself as a viable option to end pain. It takes considerable open-heartedness and patience on the part of others to withstand the teenager's negation of himself and of life, but without such relating the chances of creating hope in that young person are very slim. In particular, health care professionals need to be ready to enter into the kind of emotionally engaged relationship with troubled young people that will foster hope rather than hopelessness.

Young people who manifest depression, high anxiety and suicidal ideation have not emerged from the womb with any of these internal experiences. What leads to young people feeling invisible is the nature of the relationships they encounter within the important holding worlds of family, school and community. It is crucial to understand that those adults who have charge of children and young people can provide the holdings required to maintain their young charges' aliveness and a sense of being lovable only from the place of safe holding of themselves. Many of the significant adults in a teenager's personal life – parents, teachers, child-minders, grandparents – may have only a tentative holding of themselves and may have developed strong substitute behaviours such as addictions to substances or addictions to work, success or caring for others. Such adults do not have the maturity that is necessary to love, inspire and empower children and teenagers and, yet, there is no preventative strategy in place in our society to offset the devastating effects such immaturity can have on young people's wellbeing.

The word 'prevention' means 'to stop the coming of' and while there is no doubt that all adults possess the good intentions of maintaining young people's sense of self and excitement about life and of preventing a plunge into the darkness of despair and hopelessness, yet good intentions can be activated only from a solid interiority among the significant adults in young people's lives. When such self-realisation and confidence are not present, it is incumbent on society to provide safe holding through the provision of training opportunities not only for parents but for child-minders, pre-school teachers, and primary, secondary and third-level teachers; training that will enable them to reflect upon their own inner worlds and empower them to enter relationships characterised by love, respect, equality, understanding and compassion. All of us in society have a responsibility to provide the kind of holding worlds that give priority not to examinations or to career and economic 'success' but to psycho-social-spiritual wellbeing.

Endings: Letting go and leave-taking

- Letting go and leave-taking: Two sides of the coin of maturity
- Letting go: The primary challenge of parenting
- Leave-taking starts in childhood
- Teenagers who baulk at leave-taking
- Immature patterns of leave-taking
- Mature leave-taking

Letting go and leave-taking: Two sides of the coin of maturity

The more that individuals hold on to each other, the more likely it is that conflict will arise in the relationship; this conflict wisely bringing attention to the need for resolution of the relationship stranglehold. The more individuals let go of each other, the more likely it is that the relationship will deepen and endure. Self-possession is the key to happy relationship with another. Teenagers trying to reach for self-possession need help with such a big challenge. The best help a parent can give is to find her own self-possession. The key message that pertains in the mature relationship is, 'I'll take charge of my wellbeing, and you'll take charge of your wellbeing, and we support one another in taking on that crucial responsibility.' When this is the message that pertains, the two people can meet each other in a clear, straightforward way.

There is often an expectation that when children come into their late teens, this will be the best time for family relationships, but often this expectation is not borne out. What often passes for relationship is in fact enmeshment. Enmeshment comes from insecurity; it comes when the person is too unsafe to stand clearly in her own space, to be seen clearly and openly as her own unique, individual self – someone who can firmly and actively take charge of her own wellbeing. Letting go and leave-taking are not about endings; on the contrary, these processes are two sides of the mature coin of separateness, a process that is essential in all relationships and, in particular, the relationship between parents and teenagers. One of the primary tasks of parenting is to let go of your son or daughter and for that son or daughter to take their leave of their parents. When parents have not let go, the leave-taking by young people is unlikely to happen, or it may happen but in an atmosphere of conflict and consternation. Difficulty in letting go reflects the parents' lack of self-possession and their protection of attempting to find security by living their lives through their children or getting their children to live their lives for them – tragic time-bombs of co-dependence that may take a long time to explode but when they do explode cause very painful consequences.

One of the major challenges facing us in society – a challenge echoed on every page of this book – is that parents, teachers and other significant adults in the lives of young people need to know themselves intimately and when they do not do so this legacy of low self-esteem is passed on to the young people. In the words of Kofi Annan, a former Secretary General of the United Nations, 'We have become adept at exploring outer space, but have not developed similar skills in exploring our own personal inner spaces.'

Letting go: The primary challenge of parenting

Letting go is not about physical and emotional detachment by parents from their young adult children; on the contrary, it is about a deepening of relationship, whereby the parents now relate to the young people from a place of their own aloneness and wholeness, with respect for the place of aloneness and wholeness in the young person. This is the true homecoming that both parents and young people deserve and that is required for maturity for all to emerge. This kind of relating means that in any interaction between parents and their young adult teenagers fullness is experienced and each, having experienced the fullness of the other, walks away from the contact feeling an even deeper fullness. For this letting go – this mature separation – to happen, parents need first to have come home to themselves. When they have not, conflict will arise in the relationship with their son or daughter to draw attention to the inner work that is needed. When parents do not have a consciousness of their own insecurities, they may find themselves blaming the young person for being ungrateful, difficult and unreasonable when they attempt to take leave of their parents. In many ways, if letting go is about parents recognising and affirming the right of their teenagers to live their own lives and to be responsible for their self and for all their actions, leave-taking is about young people also becoming conscious of these same dynamics. Whether or not parents are ready, young adults need to engage in leave-taking but, of course, it makes it so much easier when parents are engaging in the process of letting go at the same time. When parents are not ready to let go, young adults may need to seek support outside the family for this essential process of leave-taking.

Leave-taking starts in childhood

The dual processes of letting go and leave-taking best happen while teenagers are still living at home. Parents need to begin as soon as possible to treat them as adults and pass responsibility for their lives onto them; they also need to maintain definite boundaries when young people resist responsibility and want to remain dependent. The process is primarily emotional in nature – it is about the creation of emotional space in the parent-young adult relationship – but it is also behavioural and social in nature. For example, behaviourally, the young adult will be expected to take responsibility for her own physical care, for her own space and possessions, for getting herself up on time in the morning and for her studies. On the social front, the young adult will be expected to take on the responsibility for how she relates to others and the consequences that follow when that relating is immature – for example, being rude or aggressive, failing to keep appointments, breaking a date or turning up late for a class. It is important that parents do not step in and take over – this deprives the young person of formative learning experiences and it perpetuates an unhealthy enmeshment. Learning from mistakes and failures is critical to leave-taking. The emotional shift that is required in the letting go and leave-taking is that the relationship moves from being a parent-child towards being an adult-adult relationship. Parenting is for children, not young adults! The adult-adult contact creates the space for the teenager to become her own person and for her to get to know her parents as individuals in their own right. So many sons and daughters never get to know their parents for the unique individuals they are and never get to hear their unique stories; this can only happen when separateness defines the relationship with their parents and their parents with them.

The behaviours that are characteristic of parents who let go include:

- unconditional love
- uninterrupted listening
- interest (as opposed to intrusion) in the young adult's life
- direct and clear communication
- requests (rather than demands or commands)
- expressions of concern from an 'I' place
- respect for (not necessarily agreement with) the young adult's beliefs, values and opinions
- modelling of independence
- acceptance of (again, not necessarily agreement with) the young adult's decisions
- definite and clear boundaries around own responsibilities
- definite and clear boundaries around not taking on the young adult's responsibilities
- willingness to offer support when the young person is struggling.

If the young adult has had predictable and consistent experiences of such mature parental behaviours from her earliest years – in an age-appropriate way – then, the ground has been well prepared, and the young adult will respond in a reciprocal mature way. If the ground for separateness has not been prepared over the years from infancy to adulthood, there will be 'weeping and gnashing of teeth' in the face of the challenges of letting go and leave-taking.

Teenagers who baulk at leave-taking

Parents can encounter the situation where the young adult refuses to take on her appropriate responsibilities. In our practice, we have heard complaints from parents that, for example, a daughter just will not apply for some course, or find some work or even help about the house. Parents need to keep perspective and not allow the presenting issue to overshadow the deeper hidden reality that somehow their daughter or son is stuck in some child-place and is very frightened of change. Threats, brow-beating or doing things for young people that they need to do for themselves will not empower them. What may touch, and consequently enable, the young person are expressions of genuine concern, unconditional love, an enquiry into how she is managing the presenting burning issue and an offer of support. Patience is essential; any pushing, any intrusion – no matter how well-intentioned – will backfire. The parent needs to listen, support, encourage and wait. If nothing happens, the parent needs to bear in mind that the young person's stuck place does not reflect on the parent but reflects the inner distress in the young person. The young person is the only one who can lead the way into her unexpressed inner turmoil; any attempt to 'pull it out of her' or expressions of exasperation will only add to the young person's anguish. If she remains unforthcoming, parents need to maintain hope and maintain the quest of finding an understanding of the young person's story – within and without the family – and make connections between how she is now and how she has been related to over the years. Parents, and other siblings, need to do their utmost not to be aggressive with or label the young adult as 'lazy', 'no good', 'manipulative', 'mad', 'bad' – all of these reactions are mirrors of inner turmoil within the labellers themselves, and when inner turmoil meets inner turmoil, conflict escalates.

Parents, in particular, need to model what they are asking of the young person – they need to take responsibility and, if necessary, go for help for themselves when they find themselves faltering in their responsibilities. While the young adult is struggling, parents need to maintain boundaries and not collude with the young person's defensive behaviours but to do so in the kindest possible way. It is in our nature to want to progress and when parents manage the situation with kindness and maturity, a breakthrough will occur for the young person. The breakthrough may be the first step and parents can expect progress to be 'one step forward, two steps back' in the dual process of leave-taking and letting go. When a young person is exhibiting alarming signs of distress – such as those described in Chapters 11, 12 and 13 – outside professional help is required but seeking such help has to be the decision of the young person. If the young person refuses to seek help, the parents can express their concern for her welfare and let her know that they intend to seek help for themselves.

Immature patterns of leave-taking

Leave-taking and physically leaving the home are not synonymous. The young person may geographically be at the other side of the world and still be emotionally enmeshed with her parents. On the other hand, the young person may still be living in the parental home and yet be relating in an independent and self-possessed manner.

The more typical pattern of leave-taking is start-stop-start. Nowadays, when teenagers finish second-level education, many of them take what has become known as a 'gap year' where they go abroad. However, this physical leave-taking does not always mean that a mature leave-taking has taken place. More often than not, when the young people return home they are still in a dependent place – as are some of their parents. It is in their relating – to themselves and others – that both parents and young adults demonstrate maturity.

Some young people leave home *prematurely* and then find themselves, for example, going back home very frequently, making frequent or even daily phone or e-mail contact when away or returning home and giving up their training or their studies or their work completely. In such situations, the young person is at the very early stages of independence and requires the opportunities and safe holding from parents that will allow her to discover her own inner stronghold.

Sometimes, the young person transfers her dependence onto a peer or an older person and becomes obsessed with this relationship. Both parties to this lean-to relationship require help to separate out from each other, but this is best coming from themselves. Generally, it is not safe for parents to voice fears and concerns as these are likely to be interpreted as interference and disapproval of the other party in the relationship. The wisdom is for parents to tread warily and stay on the sidelines until support is requested.

A not uncommon form of leave-taking is the stormy and rebellious one. The young person may accuse her parents – and others – of not understanding her, of being over-controlling, of not ever wanting what she wanted, and may be vociferous in declaring how she can do without them. Certainly, in this situation it is necessary for each parent to examine the nature of the relationship each has had and currently has with the unhappy young person. From the young person's point of view, rebelliousness is not a mature leave-taking and results in her engaging in the very co-dependent behaviours which she resents in her parents. Unless she resolves her inner issues, she will go on to create relationships with others that will be troubled. It can be helpful here if one or both parents can own and be open about aspects of their behaviour that may have contributed to her unhappiness. Apologising and offering love and support can often break the deadlock and initiate the beginnings of an adult-adult relationship between parents and young person.

There are other young adults who, though they leave home, pursue their studies, develop careers, create intimate relationships, get married and have children, continue to remain enmeshed with one or both parents. When they phone or visit the home of origin, they regress to a child-parent relationship. These young people are not in possession of self, they feel responsible for their parents and dare not do or say anything or hold beliefs or values that would cause them upset. Clearly, this can only happen when the parents collude with this enmeshment and neither a mature letting go nor leave-taking has taken place. Of course, this enmeshment with parents can have devastating effects when the young person marries and becomes a parent herself; the cycle of enmeshment is repeated and the new generation of individuals are inhibited from inhabiting their uniqueness. It can take a crisis or some outside force to rock the boat of this unhealthy enmeshment; an enmeshment that is often reinforced under the banner of 'keeping the family together'. But there is no real togetherness in enmeshment; rather all involved are tethered and fearful.

There is also the very sad and severe enmeshment where the young adult neither physically nor emotionally ever takes leave and one or other of the parents never lets go. This 'adult child' remains at home all her life and protectively believes that it is her responsibility 'to look after' one or both parents. Any attempt to create a life or a relationship outside the home can result in such reactions as harsh criticism or the parent 'taking to the bed'. The young person is helplessly entrapped and knows too well the dangers of any attempted escape. Very often siblings collude with the entrapped situation in a defensive attempt to avoid being burdened by the highly dependent parent.

Mature leave-taking

The behaviours that characterise mature leave-taking include:

- consciousness of the young person being a person in his/her own right
- consciousness that each parent is a person in his/her own right
- responsibility for self and one's own actions
- decisiveness
- risk-taking
- respect for one's own developing beliefs and values
- determination to live one's own life
- a need for time for the self
- seeing separateness as critical to all relationships
- respect for parents' own values and beliefs
- fearlessness
- spontaneity
- confidence
- security
- whole-hearted involvement in life
- active listening
- unconditional relating
- clear and definite boundaries
- supportiveness
- understanding
- flexibility
- tolerance
- kindness
- seeking support when needed.

Leave-taking is a life-time process; what is vital is that young people are provided with the safeties and the opportunities to launch themselves into the most important holding world of all – the self as the holding world.

The repeated theme throughout the book is that adults can provide a safe passage for teenagers only when they operate from their own solid interiority; finding and acting from this solid interiority is also a life-time's work.

References

Assagioli, R. (2000). *Psychosynthesis*, Amherst, MA: Synthesis Centre Publishing.

Bentall, R. (2009). *Doctoring the Mind, Why Psychiatric Treatments Fail*, London: Allen Lane.

Chopra, D. (1997). *The Path to Love*, London: Rider.

Eckersley, R. (1995). 'Values and Visions: youth and the failure of modern Western culture', *Youth Studies Australia*, Vol. 27, No. 3: 10–13.

Healy Walls, C. (2007). *The Conscious Parent*, Dublin: Original Writing Ltd.

Hersch, P. (1999). *A Tribe Apart: A Journey into the Heart of American Adolescence*, New York: Ballantine.

Higher Education Authority (2010). *A Study of Progression in Irish Higher Education*, Dublin: HEA.

Humphreys, T. and Ruddle, H. (2010). *The Compassionate Intentions of Illness*, Cork: Cork University Press.

Hyde, A., Carney, M., Drennan, J., Butler, M., Lohan, M. and Howlett, E. (2009). *Parents' Approaches to Educating their Pre-Adolescent and Adolescent Children about Sexuality*, Dublin: Crisis Pregnancy Agency.

Kelly, L., and Regan, L. (2001). *Teenage Tolerance, The Hidden Lives of Young Irish People*, Dublin: Women's Aid.

Orbach, S. (2009). *Bodies*, London: Profile Books Ltd.

Reader's Digest (2004). Survey of teenager's views of their parents.

Sullivan, C., Arensman, E., Keeley, H., Corcoran, P. and Perry, I. (2004). *Young People's Mental Health: A Report of the Results from the Lifestyle and Coping Survey*, Cork: The National Suicide Research Foundation.

Timimi, S. and Radcliffe, N. (2005). 'The Rise and Rise of ADHD'. In Craig Newnes and Nick Radcliffe (eds), *Making and Breaking Children's Lives*, UK: PCCS Books.

Whitaker, R. (2010). *Anatomy of an Epidemic*, New York: Crown Publishers.

Williamson, M. (1992): *Return to Love*, UK: Harper Collins.

INDEX